LILACS
for the garden

LILACS
for the garden

Jennifer Bennett

FIREFLY BOOKS

A FIREFLY BOOK

Published by Firefly Books Ltd. 2002

First Printing 2002

Publisher Cataloging-in-Publication Data (U.S.)

Bennett, Jennifer.
   Lilacs for the garden / Jennifer Bennett. – 1st ed.
[128] p. : col. photos. ; cm.
Includes index.
Summary: A complete guide to lilacs: planning, planting, pruning, landscaping, history and lilac aid to troubleshoot any lilac problems.
ISBN 1-55297-580-0
ISBN 1-55297-562-2 (pbk.)
1. Lilacs.   2. Gardens, Fragrant.   3. Ornamental shrubs.
I. Title.
635.968   21   CIP   SB454.3.B46   2002

**National Library of Canada Cataloguing
in Publication Data**

Bennett, Jennifer
   Lilacs for the garden

Includes index.
ISBN 1-55297-580-0 (bound)
ISBN 1-55297-562-2 (pbk.)

1. Lilacs. I. Title.

SB413.L65B45 2002   635.9'3387   C2001-903914-X

Published in the United States in 2002 by
Firefly Books (U.S.) Inc.
P.O. Box 1338, Ellicott Station
Buffalo, New York 14205

Published in Canada in 2002 by
Firefly Books Ltd.
3680 Victoria Park Avenue
Willowdale, Ontario M2H 3K1

Produced by
Bookmakers Press Inc.
12 Pine Street
Kingston, Ontario K7K 1W1
(613) 549-4347
tcread@sympatico.ca

Design by
Janice McLean

Front Cover: © Jennifer Bennett
Back Cover: all images © Jennifer Bennett

Printed and bound in Canada by
Friesens
Altona, Manitoba

Printed on acid-free paper

The Publisher acknowledges the financial support of the Government of Canada through the Book Publishing Industry Development Program for its publishing activities.

Dedication

True passion for life, for any aspect of creation, is a rare and wonderful thing. This book is dedicated to three people whose passion is the lilac, its beauty, variability and possibility, its history that is woven into our own.

The first is Isabella Preston (1881-1965) who, while employed by the federal government of Canada, developed an impressive new group of hybrid lilacs named the Prestons in her honor.

The second is John Fiala (1924-1990), Ohio clergyman, psychologist, eminent lilac breeder and author of the weighty *Lilacs: The Genus Syringa*. Fiala's enthusiasm is communicated in every page of a book dotted with exclamations such as "*Mon ami*, you must have it in your garden!" And yes, *mon ami*, I do have one of his lilacs in my garden, the golden-leafed 'Kum-Bum.'

The third is Freek Vrugtman of Ontario, an unassuming man who, as the world's registrar for lilac names, learned more about lilacs than almost anyone. Until recently, he worked at the Royal Botanical Gardens in Ontario, an inspiring place to study lilacs because it has one of the world's largest and most beautifully displayed collections. Vrugtman's most recent *International Register of Cultivar Names in the Genus Syringa*, published in 2001, is almost 400 pages of meticulously recorded and generously shared expertise.

These three people represent hundreds of men and women who have dedicated time, energy and love to this most evocative of plants. To their passion for the lilac, I owe the completion of this book.

Contents

Seasons in the Sun

A shrub for today, tomorrow and yesterday

"EVEN WITH THE CASUAL ATTENTION WE HAVE GIVEN IT,
THE LILAC IS THE OLDEST AND BEST-LOVED AMERICAN SHRUB."
— John C. Wister, *House and Garden* (1934)

Plant a lilac, and you plant a memory. Lilacs are the flowers of reminiscence, perhaps because of their fragrance, so linked for us with winter gone and summer coming, perhaps because of their brief season of fabulous bloom or perhaps because our grandparents grew them. Whatever the reason, you can ask almost anyone how they like lilacs, and they will tell you about lilacs past.

What this means is that lilacs aren't trendy. Drive through the flashiest, priciest suburbs, past the newest condos and townhouses, and you'll be lucky to see a lilac at all. You might see geometric cedars, big hydrangeas, magnolias, weeping mulberries, the colorful leaves of euonymus and spiraea and, where weather permits, azaleas, camellias and Japanese maples. But not lilacs. Most of them are down the road in the gardens of a generation or two ago, in the downscale older part of town. Some have been allowed to sucker and stretch; others have been pruned, the stubs of branches showing the rings of their age.

It seems a contradiction. Even as the choices among lilacs climb into the hundreds, they've been eclipsed as shrubs of fashion. Why? Grow them next to the townhouse plantings, and you'll see. Lilacs lack the in-your-face brilliance of azaleas, the precision of trimmed evergreens, the over-the-top profusion of hydrangeas and rhododendrons, the tropical seduction of magnolias. From a distance, lilac flowers are a haze of color. Lilacs are more subtle than many other flowering shrubs, appreciated more by the nose than by the eyes. Only close-up do you see their beauty, the profusion of petals, the singles and doubles, the colors that shift as bud opens into flower. When their blooming season is done, they fade into obscurity. For a generation raised to believe that beauty and youth go on forever, lilacs are reminders of the brevity of both.

All of which, I think, makes the lilac the perfect shrub for today's discerning gardener. A lilac forms a relationship with its owner. No other tall shrub will perfume your evenings so sweetly, reminding you to slow down, to live for just this moment as people did centuries ago. No other will promise you something to remember decades from now, when the ephemeral bursting of May will recall the perfume of lilacs by your door.

Considering the Lilacs

From Old World to New with a French connection

"THESE ARE WELL-KNOWN HARDY SHRUBS WHICH GROW WELL EVERYWHERE, IN EVERY SOIL AND ALL EXPOSURES."
— D.W. Beadle, *Canadian Fruit Flower and Kitchen Gardener* (1872)

Everywhere. Every soil. All exposures. Consider the lilacs of the field, how they grow. They are not fertilized, nor are they pruned, yet Solomon in all his glory was not arrayed like one of these. Come May, the Bible is paraphrased in abandoned farm fields and along country roads in eastern Ontario, where I live. This is lilac country, where for two weeks in spring, the abundance of flower and perfume has to be experienced to be believed. And like sleek pets looking over the fence at their wilder kin, there are lilacs in almost every garden showing off bigger blooms and brighter colors before, during and after the roadside show.

The lilac was once called the poor man's flower. The reason was that common lilacs were the chain letters of horticulture: You simply pried a rooted shoot from the base of a shrub and planted it somewhere else—just about anywhere else. Even mature lilacs could be moved. More than two centuries ago, George Washington wrote in his journal, "Removed two pretty large and full grown Lilacs to the No. Garden gate, one on each side, taking up as much dirt with the roots as cd. be well obtained." Lilacs tolerate drought, cold winters, dry, hot summers

and almost any soil. They are undemanding and generous, the perfect guests. Thanks to lilac tenacity, they grow splendidly and abundantly—sometimes too abundantly—from northern Canada to Colorado, as tough as the settlers who brought them. The lilac is the state flower of New Hampshire because, according to historian Leon Anderson, it is "symbolic of that hardy character of the men and women of the Granite State."

Lilacs flourish as though they've always been here, but their time on this continent has been brief. As Ernest H. Wilson of the Arnold Arboretum in Massachusetts said about lilacs, "None are indigenous in America, but notwithstanding this, all the species introduced have proved hardy in the arboretum. A singular and most interesting fact." Lilacs simply happen to like it here, all 20-odd species of them.

LILAC IMMIGRANTS

Most lilacs traveled a very long way to get here. The lion's share is native to mountainous regions of Asia from Afghanistan through China to Japan. Two species come from eastern Europe, one of which is the

Variegated lilac foliage in a bouquet with 'Sensation,' bottom, 'Znamya Lenina,' center, and 'Hers,' left.

A cluster of florets on one of the naturalized Syringa vulgaris *shrubs that create a springtime show along rural roadsides.*

ancestor of our common roadside lilac, *Syringa vulgaris.* In its native territory, however, the common lilac may not look like our naturalized one. Edgar Anderson wrote about the wild European lilacs in the Arnold Arboretum bulletin: "Their flowers are not borne in bunches but in great open sprays. The panicles may reach two feet in length. Nor does the general form of the bush follow closely a single pattern, as in the cultivated lilac." Cultivated lilacs, selections that were made unknown centuries ago, are the shrubs that run wild in North America.

About five centuries ago, *S. vulgaris* made its way westward from its home in the Balkans—garden by garden, perhaps—to the Atlantic. France, long enamored of perfumes, embraced it so fondly and transformed it so beautifully that in the common parlance, all *S. vulgaris* cultivars can be called French hybrids,

no matter their origin. Granted *savoir faire*, the common lilac went forth renewed with larger clusters of bigger florets, sometimes double, and not just colored lilac or white but in hues of pale pink and pinkish blue through violet, magenta and purple. Fragrant flowers covered the shrubs from head to toe.

When lilacs arrived in England, they were called pipe trees in honor of their hollow stems. In his 17th-century herbal, John Parkinson wrote about one type of pipe tree that bore "blew or violet coloured flowers on a long stalke, of the bignesse and fashion of a Foxe taile." There were an additional "two or three sorts," including one with silver flowers, another with single white flowers and yet another with cut leaves. According to English legend, the white-flowered type arose from lilac-colored blooms pressed into the soil of the grave of a beloved young woman. By the next fall, the

Lilacs are tough; these flourish in the shallow soil next to exposed bedrock despite competition from neighboring trees.

branches had rooted and were blooming white.

Around the time of Parkinson's herbal, the common lilac came ashore in North America in the baggage of settlers. Its offspring prosper. Some of the original immigrants, now more than 250 years old, still grow on Mackinac Island, Michigan. "You can pick the flowers from a second-story window," says Bruce Peart, curator of the lilac collection at the Royal Botanical Gardens in Ontario.

Syringa vulgaris was followed to this continent by a parade of exotic *Syringa* species, most discovered during the competitive age of plant exploration called by one Victorian "the era of Omnium Gatherum." For two centuries starting around the mid-1700s, botanical explorers brought home thousands of now everyday garden plants, including magnolias, rhododendrons, forsythias, mock oranges and lilacs. It was a no-holds-barred era

for searching, uprooting and shipping. From China came S. *pekinensis* in the mid-1700s, S. *oblata* in 1856, S. *pubescens* in 1880 and S. *villosa* in 1889. The largest lilac collections were gathered in St. Petersburg, Paris, the Arnold Arboretum in the United States and Kew Gardens in England.

"Come down to Kew in lilac time,
in lilac time, in lilac time.
Come down to Kew in lilac time
(it isn't far from London!)"
—Alfred Noyes, "The Barrel Organ"

As the years passed, collecting became increasingly discriminating and legislated. Most impressive was the collecting done for the Arnold Arboretum, especially by Ernest Henry Wilson (1876-1930), a scholarly ad-

Capable of living hundreds of years, lilacs can eventually develop thick branches that exhibit a spiral growth pattern.

venturer who has been called the Indiana Jones of the plant world. From 1902 to 1926, Wilson collected hundreds of plants of many species in China, including lilacs he discovered and some that were rare but had been previously described by other scientists.

THE CREATORS

Neither plant breeders nor gardeners are content with what is, so the lilacs that arrived from eastern Europe and Asia were not only studied but also selected and hybridized. Patience is a necessary virtue in developing new lilacs. The genus is amenable enough to having its pollen moved from flower to flower, but the breeder won't see the results of his or her meddling for several years—not until the baby flowers. Nevertheless, more than 240 patient people have, during the past couple of centuries in Europe, Russia and especially North

America, turned their attention to the genus *Syringa*. By 1900, there were 300 lilac cultivars worldwide; by 1960, they numbered 830. There are now close to 4,000, although you won't find most of them in a plant nursery. Most were produced in small numbers, and some are lost, likely flourishing unlabeled in the gardens of their creators and their friends. But a few are probably at your local nursery, and hundreds are available from lilac specialists. Compared with wild lilacs, these newer varieties may offer gardeners greater disease resistance, larger flowers with more intense colors, double flowers and a longer blooming season. Sizes range from knee-high shrubs to trees as tall as a three-story building.

The oldest way to obtain improvements is known as selection, the method that produced a few ancient lilacs found in Asian and eastern European gardens. Selection is still a perfectly worthy, though slow, way to a better

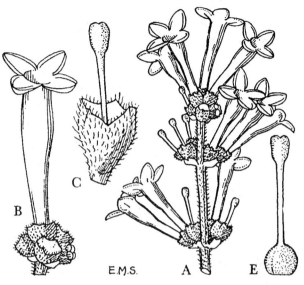

Isabella Preston, immortalized by her line of Preston lilacs, was one of many plant breeders interested in the genus. From a cluster of florets, B, they isolate an individual inflorescence, A, and its components, the calyx, style and stigma, C. E reveals the basal ovary, where new seeds—perhaps hybrids—will develop.

lilac. From a group of plants grown in the wild or in cultivation, one simply chooses the best and then propagates it by cloning, creating genetic copies of the parent plant. Selection might produce a subtle improvement or a more dramatic mutation, also known as a sport.

For the past century, the usual way to create new cultivars has been by cross-pollination, physically transporting the pollen from the anther, the male part of one flower, to the stigma, the female part of another flower, then ensuring that no further pollination occurs. The resulting seeds must be sown and grown to flowering stage for the results to be known. Typically, hundreds of seedlings are grown before a lilac improvement is selected, and as beauty is in the eye of the beholder, this may or may not be perceived as an improvement beyond the garden gate of the creator.

Of all the hundreds of lilac breeders, the following have had the greatest impact on the development of the genus.

The Lemoine Family: Victor Lemoine of Nancy, France, was the first person to hybridize lilacs in an organized and extensive fashion. In the 19th century, he and his wife Marie created the first large-flowered double lilacs and the *hyacinthiflora* hybrids. Their work, mostly with *S. vulgaris*, was carried on by their son Emile and grandson Henri until the nursery closed in 1955. Many of the more than 200 Lemoine lilacs are still easy to find and considered excellent. They include doubles such as deep blue 'Président Grévy' (1886), white 'Mme Lemoine' (1890), pink 'Belle de Nancy' (1891), dark magenta 'Charles Joly' (1896), lilac 'Léon Gambetta' (1907), white 'Miss Ellen Willmott' (1903) and rose-pink 'Paul Thirion' (1915).

The Rochester Lilacs: John Dunbar was a Scotsman who, in the 1890s, created the famous lilac gardens at Highland Park in Rochester, New York, now the home of an annual lilac festival (see Sources). He introduced the blue-purple 'President Lincoln' (1916), not only one of the most popular American lilacs of all time but also a good choice as a parent. His other most widely available cultivars are the single pale lilac 'General Sherman' (1917) and purple 'President Roosevelt' (1919). Doubles include the deep purple 'Adelaide Dunbar' (1916) and the white 'Joan Dunbar' (1923). Working later at the same park, horticulturist Alvan Grant developed, from Lemoine's 'Edith Cavell,' the single white 'Rochester' (1971), most famous for its extensive use as a breeding parent for progeny such as the blue 'Dwight D. Eisenhower' and violet-purple 'Flower City,' both selected by Richard Fenicchia, horticulturist at the park from 1950 to 1978. Some of the Rochester lilacs are distinguished by upright clusters of single flowers that are multi-petaled—each petal is divided—and by colors that resist fading in bright sun.

Isabella Preston (1881-1965): This horticulturist has a special place in lilac history as the first woman to make important breeding advances at a time—the 1920s—when it was difficult for women to obtain paid employment in the sciences at all. Preston studied horticulture in England, then in Canada at the Ontario Agricultural College before she became employed at the Central Experimental Farm in Ottawa. There, she created a line of hybrids called the Preston lilacs (*S.* x *prestoniae*), which are tall, late-blooming, disease-resistant and very winter-hardy, to zone 2 or 3. She chose most of her cultivar names, such as 'Desdemona' and 'Juliet,' from Shakespeare. Preston also officially described the hybrid *S.* x *josiflexa* and created outstanding varieties of roses, crabapples, mock oranges and lilies. There is a collection of Preston lilacs at the Royal Botanical Gardens in Ontario and another at the Central Experimental Farm, where she worked. Preston died in 1965 at the age of 85.

Frank L. Skinner (1882-1967): A Manitoba cattle rancher, Skinner became interested in developing ornamental plants that could withstand the rigors of the Canadian prairies and taught himself the science of plant breeding. His Hardy Plant Nursery became world-famous as a source of his own fruit trees and ornamentals, including lilies, roses and lilacs—144 introductions in all. The "Luther Burbank of Canada" made his greatest impression upon the genus *Syringa* with what he called "American lilacs" such as the enduringly popular 'Maiden's Blush,' winter-hardy, early-blooming *S.* x *hyacinthiflora* hybrids of *S. vulgaris* x *S. oblata* subsp. *dilatata*. The Skinner Nursery, now in Roblin, Manitoba, sells several of his lilacs (ships only to Canada; see Sources).

Dr. William Cumming (1911-1999): Skinner's brother-in-law, Cumming was an employee of the Agriculture Canada experimental station in Morden, Manitoba, when he developed many noteworthy cold-hardy ornamentals. Among lilacs, he created inter-species hybrids such as the dwarf cultivars 'Minuet' and 'Miss Canada,' the latter such an unusual bright pink that it is simply called the Pink Lilac.

Leonid Kolesnikov (1893-1974): Lilacs have taken to the soil of Russia just as they have to the similarly harsh Canadian prairies and the American Midwest. An outstanding Russian horticulturist, Kolesnikov developed subtleties in lilac coloration unmatched by anyone else. One of the most highly praised lilacs on the market today is his 'Krasavitsa Moskvy' (Beauty of Moscow) of 1947, which has double white flowers tinged with pink and lilac. This variety, along with his single purple-lilac 'Znamya Lenina' (Banner of Lenin) and his double bluish lilac 'Nadezhda' (Hope), are considered three of the best lilacs in the world by Ted "Doc Lilac" Collins of Rochester, New York. 'Mechta,' also widely available, has very large single bluish lilac flowers.

University of New Hampshire: From this plant-breeding program has come one of the most sought-after lilacs of the end of the 20th century—*S. pubescens* subsp. *patula* 'Miss Kim,' released by Albert F. Yeager (1892-1961). Also outstanding from that university are several *S.* x *josiflexa* lilacs sometimes classified as Prestons: 'Anna Amhoff' and 'James Macfarlane,' both from Yeager, and 'Agnes Smith,' from contemporary horticulturist Dr. Owen Rogers.

John Fiala (1924-1990): Author of *Lilacs: The Genus Syringa*, Fiala was not only a parish priest, teacher,

Rugged enough for the prairies, 'Pocahontas' is one of the hyacinth lilacs produced by Canadian Frank Skinner.

writer and one of the founding directors of the International Lilac Society but also an award-winning hybridizer who introduced about 50 named lilacs, including several that are easy to find: 'Albert F. Holden,' the dwarf 'Pixie' and 'Arch McKean.' Fiala was especially interested in the color blue and released several blue lilacs, including the remarkable pale blue 'Wedgwood Blue' and the darker 'Blue Delft' and 'Wonderblue.'

21st-Century Breeding: The lilac 'Kum-Bum' developed by John Fiala is an example of the newest turn in lilac breeding. The color of its golden leaves was achieved by exposing the seeds to the chemical colchicine. Chemicals, along with radiation and possibly genetic manipulation, may be a speedier way to reach contemporary aims: dwarf plants, interesting foliage, good fall color, brighter colors in a wider range and larger flowers that bloom over a longer period. The shrub or tree should be resistant to pests and diseases and hold its flowers out to be seen instead of hiding them under the foliage as some of the older lilacs do. Still, if a buyer wants fragrance and old-fashioned appeal, there may be nothing better than one of the heirloom lilacs that have stood the test of time.

THE BOTANICAL LILAC

Most lilacs are shrubs, but a couple are smallish trees. What's the difference? Trees are generally understood to be taller and to have one stem, although shrubs, of course, can be pruned to just one stem, so the two terms overlap.

The foliage also varies. The common lilac (*S. vulgaris*) has fairly large simple, opposite, untoothed leaves, but lesser-known species may have leaves that are lobed, compound, feathered or small. The individual flowers, called florets, are often fragrant. Florets typically have four petals and are relatively small, but they are borne in large clusters—properly called thyrses but also known as panicles or racemes—so the overall effect is showy. The flowers may be double, meaning that each individual floret has more than the usual four petals. Flowers described as "multipetals" are singles whose petals are divided. Petals may be rounded, elongated, pointed, folded, cupped or curved backward (reticulated) or forward. After the flowers fade, there remain dry brown capsules that enclose the seeds.

The lilac belongs to the family Oleaceae, the olives. Its best-known garden cousins are forsythia, jasmine, ash and privet, all of which have four-petaled flowers. So closely is lilac related to privet that it can be grafted onto privet; botanists once grouped tree lilacs with privets, *Ligustrum*. Privet flowers look like small white lilacs.

All lilacs belong to the genus *Syringa*, which is named after Syrinx, a nymph of Greek legend who was changed into a reed to escape the advances of the amorous Pan. In the circuitous manner of mythology, Pan chose that very reed, the transformed Syrinx herself, to create his Pan pipes. So the name *Syringa* suggests the plant's hollow, reedlike stems, which inspired one of its early names, pipe tree. Confusingly, "syringa" is also a common name for mock orange (*Philadelphus lewisii*). And "lilac" is used for some unrelated plants that bear clusters of bluish flowers: a couple of forms of *Ceanothus* (California lilac) and *Hardenbergia* (vine lilac) as well as *Hebe hulkeana* (New Zealand lilac).

Botanical nomenclature is a little like the Chinese system of naming humans. The "surname" goes first—in this case, *Syringa*—followed by the species name. Often, the species name is descriptive. For instance, the species name of the common lilac, *vulgaris*, resembles and means the same as the English word vulgar, or common; *S.* x *persica* denotes the supposed origin of that species in Persia; and *S. pinnatifolia* has pinnate, or feathered, foliage. Some species names honor people. *S. josikaea* commemorates the Baroness Rosalia von Josika, the botanist who brought this lilac to the attention of the scientific community. Renaming occurs as more is discovered about the plant. Among many outdated species names once commonly used and still encountered occasionally in nursery catalogs are *S. japonica*, *S. palibiniana*, *S. rothomagenesis* and *S. velutina*.

Syringa vulgaris, *the common lilac, generally bears clusters of single four-petaled florets and simple opposite leaves.*

Confusing the issue are the interspecific hybrids (hybrids between different species). When two lilac species are crossed, the female parent of the hybrid is listed first, followed by the letter "x" and then the male parent's name. If that hybrid has numerous offspring, a new species name might be created, but it must have the multiplication sign "x" in front of it. Thus hybrids of S. *villosa* x S. *reflexa* have been given a new name, S. x *prestoniae*, in honor of Isabella Preston. When Preston made the opposite cross, using S. *reflexa* as the female parent, the offspring were not as memorable.

What happens when three or more species are involved in a new hybrid? These so-called tribreds, or multibreds—such as Syringa 'Bailbelle'—may be given no species name at all. Incidentally, this cultivar has also been given the trademark name Tinkerbelle™. Trademarked or registered names, which are increasingly common and are in addition to the plant's scientific cultivar name, enable the breeder to collect revenue for the use of the name. Often these names are used to sell plants more easily in countries other than the place (and language) of origin. Thus the Russian 'Krasavitsa Moskvy' is marketed in Germany under the trademarked name Schöne von Moskau™. The English translation, Beauty of Moscow, is not trademarked.

Cultivar (cultivated variety) names such as that of S. *vulgaris* 'Agincourt Beauty' are enclosed in single quotation marks. In a plant nursery, the species or cultivar name is likely all you'll see—and all you really need to know. Cultivar names must be approved and registered to ensure that no two cultivars have the same name and that the names are appropriate in length and description. This means that everywhere it goes, a plant has the same name which it shares with no other.

A common lilac progresses from winter dormancy, LEFT, *to April bud-swelling and then through phenophases 1 and 2.*

LILAC TIME

"THE COMMON LILAC WON'T OPEN ITS BUDS UNTIL IT IS SAFE TO DO SO
(WHICH IS WHY THE FLOWERING CAN VARY BY AS MUCH AS THREE WEEKS FROM ONE SEASON TO ANOTHER),
AND THE FARMER OR GARDENER WHO TAKES PHENOLOGY FOR HIS GUIDE WILL WATCH FOR
THIS FLOWERING RATHER THAN GO BY THE BOOKS AND PERFORM CERTAIN TASKS AT A FIXED DATE."
—Eleanor Perényi, *Green Thoughts* (1981)

In her essay, Perényi explains that if Minnesota farmers wait 10 days after lilac-blooming time to harvest their alfalfa, they can eliminate the first brood of alfalfa weevils. This sort of linking of the schedules of two living things—in this case, lilac and weevil—is known as phenology. The U.S. International Biological Program Phenology Committee explains it more fully: "Phenology is the study of the timing of recurring biological events, the causes of their timing with regard to biotic and abiotic forces, and the interrelation among phases of the same or different species." Once the lilacs are in bloom, you'd better check for birch leaf miner on your birch trees, gypsy moth larvae on all kinds of deciduous trees and lilac borers right there on the lilacs.

And there is a newer reason to keep track of lilac bloom time. Climatic changes such as global warming can be tracked year by year. Mark D. Schwartz of the University of Wisconsin-Milwaukee is coordinating a continent-wide project that notes significant dates in the development of one lilac cultivar and one honeysuckle cultivar. Schwartz writes in the *International*

Journal of Biometeorology: "The results of such studies in North America have demonstrated the potential of phenology as an efficient monitor of global change throughout midlatitude regions."

The common lilac (*S. vulgaris*) is an excellent phenological indicator because it is hardy, relatively disease- and pest-resistant and passes through quite easily identifiable stages in sensitive response to the temperature of air and soil. Increasing day length has little influence—the plant is what is known as "day-neutral." The development of other plants and insects triggered by temperature can be clocked by the lilac.

From year to year, lilac bloom time can vary by more than a month—something that is an annual cause of anxiety to the organizers of lilac festivals such as the one in Rochester, New York, where the earliest peak bloom time was April 29, 1945, and the latest June 8, 1924. Their sensitivity to temperature means that lilacs near warm south-facing walls bloom earlier than do lilacs in the field.

There are five well-defined phenophases (stages used in phenology) in lilac development:

In eastern Ontario, phenophase 3, LEFT, *usually occurs in mid-May and full bloom a week later,* THIRD FROM LEFT.

1. first leaf, when the widest part of the green leaf is showing past the brown bud tips

2. fully or 95 percent leafed

3. first bloom, when at least 50 percent of the flower clusters have at least one flower open

4. full bloom, about a week later, when 95 percent of the flower clusters no longer have any unopened flowers but before many have withered

5. end of bloom, when at least 95 percent of the flowers have withered or dried up.

Keep track of these dates in your own garden from year to year to determine climatic patterns and dates of related events.

In the 1960s, researchers at the University of Ver- mont set up a network of volunteers to record the dates of the five phenophases. The network, which has since extended throughout the northeast, has shown that stage 1 is a good time to plant cool-weather crops such as lettuce, peas and carrots, while stage 4 is the time to sow warm-weather crops such as beans and cucumbers.

Home gardeners who live where winters are cold enough for timely lilac-bud development are some- times invited to participate in phenology surveys. The *S. vulgaris* cultivar 'Charles Joly' is a popular subject, as is *S. x chinensis* 'Red Rothomagensis.' If you are inter- ested, search the World Wide Web under the subject "phenology."

AND EAT IT TOO

Lilac flowers are edible, just like violas, roses, hollyhocks, daylilies and many others. Sample lilac flow- ers before using them, as some kinds are tastier than others. Pick the flowers soon after they open, wash them if they are dusty, let them dry, then pick off individual florets to use in salads or desserts or as gar- nishes on the plate. Plant explorer Joseph Hers recorded almost a cen- tury ago that the flowers of the

littleleaf lilac (*S. pubescens* subsp. *microphylla*) were used in China to make a tea.

Lilacs, or pipe trees, have appar- ently also been used medicinally. In his 1629 herbal, John Parkinson wrote, "We have no use of these in Physicke that I know, although Prosper Alpinus saith the double white Pipe tree is much used in Egypt to help women in their tra- vailes of childbirth."

A woodcut of a pipe tree—the common lilac—appears in John Parkinson's 17th-century herbal of useful plants.

Planning, Planting and Pruning

Selecting and growing garden lilacs

"The lilac is popular throughout the world, but I believe that nowhere
is it as beautiful as in the United States and Canada. In those countries,
the contrast between the dry warm summers and the very vigorous winters lends itself
wonderfully to the development of the lilac and the richness of its bloom."
—Emile Lemoine in Alice Harding's *Lilacs in My Garden* (1933)

A lilac can be one of the most beautiful plants in your garden, provided it makes it through two critical passages. The first is the time you spend choosing it; the second is the time you spend planting it. Give as much time and thought as you can to planning and planting, and your lilac's beauty can outlive you.

There are many things to consider when choosing a lilac. Your first will likely be color of bloom and placement in your landscape, both discussed in the next chapter. They are important, but climate is more so if you live at the edges of the best lilac areas. Climatic zones 4 through 7 are ideal for lilacs. In a trial of winter hardiness at the University of Maine (zone 4), none of the 175 or so lilac species and cultivars suffered any damage.

What are climatic zones? Both Canada and the United States have published maps that divide their territories into areas of climatic similarity. The U.S. map, which describes both countries and is thus the one used in this book, defines each zone exclusively by its average minimum winter temperature. Higher zone numbers mean milder winters (see map on page 118).

The lilac is the only fabulously varied shrub that gives the advantage of great choice to gardeners who live with long cold winters. Most lilacs require about 1,000 hours below 50 degrees F (10°C) to trigger the development of their flower buds, and they'll put up with far more cold weather than that. Lilacs give gardeners in zones 2 to 4, where 42 cool days in a row are easy to come by, the unaccustomed delight of hundreds of choices, and not only common lilacs but also the *josiflexa*, Preston and some tree lilacs as well as the rarer *Syringa villosa* and *S. wolfii*. The *hyacinthiflora* lilacs and broadleaf lilac (*S. oblata*) are tough enough, but because they bloom early, their buds can be damaged by late frost. It's important, especially at the colder edges of the zones of lilac hardiness, to plant your choices on high ground, not in frost pockets where cold air can rest. One valley lilac grower sprays the shrubs with water on frosty

Double lilacs such as 'Président Poincaré' are distinguished by individual florets that have more than four petals.

In spring, a wide selection of lilac cultivars and species can be purchased in pots from specialized nurseries.

nights near bloom time to save the buds from damage.

Most lilacs need a cold winter to bloom, but a precious few bloom quite reliably in zone 8 and even in the coolest corners of zone 9. *Syringa* x *chinensis*, *S.* x *hyacinthiflora*, *S. pubescens* subsp. *patula* and some cultivars of *S. vulgaris* will bloom in hardiness zone 8, although mildew can be unsightly where summers are humid. Southern growers have found that if they withhold water in summer to force dormancy, new growth and flowering will begin when watering resumes, even without a period of cold. (In these areas, a heat-zone map may be useful. It can be found on the website www.ars.org/publications/heat_zone_map.htm. This map divides the United States into zones according to the average number of days above 86 degrees F/30°C. Zone 1, the coolest, has just one day above that temperature, while zone 8, the warmest zone for lilacs,

charts 91 to 100 days. Heat zone 8—roughly the same geographically as hardiness zone 9, too warm for most lilacs—travels from the mountainous areas of California across northern Texas and northern Louisiana to the Atlantic. Monrovia Nursery [see Sources] gives heat-zone recommendations for its lilacs.)

Wherever you live, check the fine print in the catalog, or ask a nursery salesperson for the climatic-zone recommendations for your lilac.

My most recent lilac purchase for my zone 5 garden in eastern Ontario was in the local automotive-supplies store, where a grocery cart full of boxes on sale offered 'Hallelujah,' a lilac that John Fiala, in his classic *Lilacs: The Genus Syringa*, judged "very fine." Although the box described 'Hallelujah' as purple and Fiala assures me it will bloom magenta, I considered my bargain-basement find something of a coup. A lilac

Soil is packed around the roots of a young tree lilac.

that Fiala described as scarce was mine for less than the price of lunch. Likely your lilac choice will be similar—you'll buy what is offered locally when you happen to see it and you have some money in your pocket. But I've also bought lilacs by mail and was then able to choose at my leisure from hundreds of varieties, selecting the yellow-leafed *S. tomentella* 'Kum-Bum' and the picotee-petaled *S. vulgaris* 'Sensation.' After I'd read a bit, I picked up from local nurseries 'Miss Kim,' 'Dappled Dawn' and 'Palibin' to grow along a fence and three 'Ivory Silk' tree lilacs to plant along the sidewalk at the front of our house. One lilac had already been planted there long before (see photographs on pages 24 and 25), a wildling of *S. vulgaris* with small white flowers and the ability to sucker itself into the next millennium. Because most of it grows on the next-door neighbor's property, it is there to stay.

If you have the luxury of time, search the Internet or buy a catalog from one of the larger lilac producers. There are so many lilacs—and some so much finer than others—that it seems a shame to settle for less than lovely when a lilac is such a long-term commitment in your landscape.

WHEN TO PLANT

Lilacs are best planted in spring, as soon as the soil has thawed and is workable; don't plant them in ground that is still soggy from melted snow. At the Royal Botanical Gardens in southern Ontario (zone 6), the favored planting time is the second half of April. This early planting allows the roots to begin growing before summer's heat and drought. Spring is also when the best selection of lilacs is available and when they will likely arrive if you are having plants shipped. On the other hand, Russian lilac breeder Leonid Kolesnikov found that lilacs transplanted well in summer, when the soil was dry. Lilacs sold in pots may be available for planting all season. Alice Harding, author of *Lilacs in My Garden* (Macmillan, 1933), moved her lilacs all year except when they were blooming. Don't leave planting too late, however. After the soil temperature drops to 41 degrees F (5°C) in fall, root growth is so slow that the plant will not become established before winter.

LILAC REQUIREMENTS

Lilacs need sun, at least four hours a day. The more, the better in northern gardens (zones 2 to 6), although in more southerly gardens, the higher and brighter the sun shines, the more appreciative lilacs are of partial shade. A bit of shade will also slow the fading of pinks and the darker colors.

Lilacs need space. The usual distance allowed between shrubs in botanical gardens and arboretums is 6 feet (1.8 m). If you are growing your lilac in a lawn and use a riding mower, 10 feet (3 m) is better. The only time closer planting is advised is for a hedge (see pages 56-57).

Lilacs need well-drained soil. With the exception of the Himalayan lilac (*S. emodi*), they will die in waterlogged ground. If you must plant where the soil is not well drained—if water tends to puddle or the ground usually feels damp in spring and cracks in summer—

raise the bed before you plant the lilac. Over the heavy shallow clay soil at the Holden Arboretum in Kirtland, Ohio, the lilac garden was prepared with 3 inches (7.5 cm) of sandy gravel covered with 9 to 12 inches (22-30 cm) of topsoil, then 3 inches (7.5 cm) of well-rotted manure. After the lilacs were planted, they were mulched with bark chips.

Provided it is well drained, virtually any soil will do, from slightly acidic to quite alkaline. Poor soil suits lilacs. In soil that is too rich or too heavily fertilized, they may not bloom. The lilac's legendary need for alkaline soil comes from tolerance—they survive on virtually bare limestone—rather than preference. But soil that is very acidic, below pH 6.5, should be amended with half a cup (125 mL) of horticultural lime mixed into the hole at planting time and spread around the base of the plant every spring.

PLANTING YOUR LILAC

Once you've located a good position—in full sun or slight shade, with well-drained soil and plenty of elbow-room in an aesthetically pleasing spot, as described in the next chapter—remove all sod and stones from the planting area, and dig a hole about 50 percent wider than the rootball; save the removed soil. The hole should be deep enough that the lilac can be planted at the same depth as before, with all roots buried. Fill the planting hole with water just before you plant your lilac.

Your lilac will arrive in one of three ways: bare-root, in a pot or wrapped in burlap (called "balled and burlapped"). Mail-order plants usually arrive bare-root. In truth, the roots are not quite bare; they are generally wrapped in damp sphagnum and stuffed into a plastic sleeve, but once you remove the moss, the roots will be bare. Don't allow them to dry out. While you dig the hole for your lilac, leave it in a bucket of cool water in the shade. If you can't plant it immediately, heel the plant into the ground by covering the roots with damp soil; water whenever the soil dries out.

Potted plants must be removed from their pots before planting. Even fiber pots should be cut or torn away. Sometimes a plant will slide easily out of the pot, but don't lift it by the stem or pull it hard because you may tear its roots. Press the sides of the pot to loosen the

Full sun, plenty of elbowroom and a wood-chip mulch provide a young lilac with a promising start, ABOVE. *A rail fence,* FACING PAGE, *creates an attractive background.*

rootball and then hold the pot at an angle or upside down while you ease the plant out. If the shrub or tree is large and especially if it is rootbound, you may need to step on the side of the pot to loosen its grip. Gently slide the plant out of the pot and lift it by putting your hands under the rootball. You may need help to keep the stem vertical while you shovel soil around the roots.

It is usually the larger lilacs that are balled and burlapped, and at least two people are needed to handle them. Burlap may be treated to resist decay, so it should be removed. Untie the burlap around the stem, lift the plant by the burlap and slide the plant into the hole. Remove any labels, twine or wire.

When the lilac roots are in position in the planting hole, fill around and over them with removed soil. Do

not add fertilizers or additives such as peat moss, as the tree will fare better in the long run if it is not planted in a pocket of superior soil, which could discourage root growth beyond the pocket. Firm the soil around the roots with your foot, then water deeply. A bucket of water per plant is about right. Don't press the wet soil down. Stake for the first year only if the planting site is very windy.

MULCHING

Whether or not to mulch is a matter of preference. Mulching keeps weeds down and holds soil moisture in. It helps prevent girdling accidents from mowers and trimmers. It looks attractive if it extends as far out as the width of the mature plant. Mulching is done at most botanical gardens, where the usual mulch is shredded bark, which can be spread directly over the weeded soil about 4 to 6 inches (10-15 cm) deep and renewed every three years. The usual labor-saving practice is to apply the grass killer 2,4-D (Roundup) directly to the circle of sod around the stem in summer or fall and immediately spread the mulch. An environmentally friendly alternative for the home garden involves spreading several layers of newspaper over the sod, then covering them with mulch. The newspaper will compost in a season, and the sod underneath will die. An alternative to bark mulch is a groundcover, a living mulch. See pages 48-50 for groundcover ideas.

For the first month, water the lilac thoroughly once a week if the weather is dry. For the remainder of the first summer, water every couple of weeks during dry weather. Lilac roots are shallow but can be encouraged to grow downward with deep watering. In the following seasons, a lilac should not require any watering unless there is a prolonged drought.

GRAFTED VS. OWN-ROOT

If your lilac has been grafted, you will see a slight swelling, a sort of "knee joint," above the roots. The bark may look different above and below this joint. Grafting is the joining of your desired lilac cultivar (called the scion) to another type of lilac used for its roots (called the stock). When you plant the lilac, the graft should be below ground to encourage the scion to

Suckers are shoots that grow quickly from the roots.

put out its own roots. Grafting of lilacs, once very common, is no longer favored for several reasons. For one thing, the rootstock is a different variety from the scion. It may be less winter-hardy or somewhat incompatible. Should shoots emerge from the rootstock, you could end up with an entirely different lilac. This is one way to determine whether a lilac already growing on your property was grafted. If the shoots arising from below the ground bear the same flowers as the older branches, your lilac was not grafted—or, just as good, has rooted from above the graft. Another problem with grafts is that they present entry spots for borers and for a fungal disease that can cause the quick decline and death of your plant.

There is one situation in which grafting is required. If you are growing a standard (see page 42), you have no choice but to accept a grafted plant. In this case, the graft is high on the stem and of course remains

Lilacs will grow without fertilizer, but profuse blooming is more likely if a low-nitrogen fertilizer is applied in June.

above ground in planting. Except for standards, lilacs grown on their own roots are the ones you should look for. Mail-order catalogs will tell you whether their lilacs are grafted. Ask your neighborhood nursery, but examine the stem to be sure.

FERTILIZING

Most garden lilacs—and all wild lilacs—survive with no fertilizing at all. Lilacs are remarkably self-sufficient and more likely to be harmed by too much fertilizer than too little. If you want to fertilize, hold off the year you plant and wait until the following spring. At the Royal Botanical Gardens, fertilizing takes place every year in June, as soon as most of the lilacs have finished blooming and have been pruned. Bruce Peart, curator of the gardens' lilac collection, says, "We use a general 'vegetable grower' fertilizer such as 4-12-8. It's

high in phosphorus. The fertilizer is cultivated in at the base of the tree and then irrigated in." Frank Moro, lilac breeder and owner of Select Plus Nursery in Quebec, suggests that home gardeners fertilize every two or three years with 5-10-5. Russian lilac expert Leonid Kolesnikov used nothing but "green water," which he made by fermenting grass clippings and weeds in water.

If you are using a commercial fertilizer, the recommended rate for shrubs is 1 to 2 pounds per 100 square feet (0.5-1 kg per 10 m²) for those grouped in beds, or 0.5 to 1 pound (0.25-0.5 kg) per plant for specimen plants. Use the lower figures in colder areas (zones 2 to 4). Apply the fertilizer lightly around the drip line— the ground directly under the farthest reaches of the branch tips. Fertilize only in spring. Water thoroughly after applying a dry fertilizer.

A long-neglected shrub, LEFT, *has had some of its largest branches cut with a saw,* CENTER, *to just above an offshoot,* RIGHT. *Over the next two years, the renovation will be completed.* FACING PAGE, *pruning shears are used for the annual routine of shaping the shrub and removing spent flowers, which will promote dense flowering and keep the shrub relatively short.*

PRUNING

"Why should I prune my lilacs?" asks a friend. "I drive through the country in May, through all the wild lilacs, and wonder, "Who prunes *those* lilacs?" It's a good question, because nobody does. Pruned or unpruned, lilacs in sun and well-drained soil will probably grow and bloom. Unpruned, they grow steadily taller, bearing their often biennial crop of flowers farther up and out until they are virtually unpickable and unprunable. They're just too tall and too choked with suckers, a natural look that may be exactly what you want on a country property.

Pruned lilacs are more likely to bloom every year and to stay a size that suits you. They'll probably be healthier, the blooming more prolific and the flower clusters larger. Dave Bakker of J.C. Bakker & Sons Nurseries in Ontario says, "People shouldn't be afraid to whack lilacs back. Otherwise they can get too big. There is a dwarf Korean lilac near me that has been allowed to grow 12 feet tall and 8 feet wide—that's a dwarf!" (This is 'Miss Kim,' reputed to mature at 5 feet/1.5 m.)

Annual pruning is essential in arboretums and public gardens, where the lilacs need to look their best every spring. In the home garden, lilacs can be pruned every year or less frequently. The less frequently you prune, the bigger and more difficult the job will eventually be. In small gardens, where space is at a premium, annual pruning is essential.

Cutting lilac flowers to bring indoors is a type of pruning, not very methodical but the right idea. When carloads of people stopped by the wild lilacs growing near our farm and took home armloads of fragrant flowers, I wondered whether they realized they were doing the shrubs as well as themselves a favor. The shrubs quickly replaced the removed vegetation with new leaf and flower buds for next spring's show.

Of course, picking flowers is too random to be a reliable pruning method. People who want cut flowers snip off only the most accessible ones. Their scissors or knives may spread disease. To do this job properly, you will need a pruning saw—preferably curved and with a strong handle—and sharp pruning shears or secateurs. For branches thicker than about an inch (2.5 cm), you may also want the leverage afforded by long-handled pruning shears. Keep your saw and pruners sharp, and disinfect them between plants in Lysol, rubbing alcohol or a fresh solution of 1 part household bleach diluted in 10 parts water.

Cut branches in one of three places: just above a bud, flush with the adjoining branch or at the ground.

On all lilacs, pruning should be done as soon after the flowers have faded as you can manage. Most people aren't too fond of the look of spent lilac flowers, so this schedule takes care of deadheading and pruning at the same time. In summer, the plant forms its buds—both leaf and flower—for the next year, so don't leave pruning so late that you end up cutting off next year's flowers. Most hardy spring-flowering shrubs, incidentally, have the habit of flowering on buds developed the previous season, so you can set aside a day for pruning not only the lilacs but also white spiraea, forsythia, mock orange (*Philadelphus*), caragana (*Caragana* spp.), ninebark (*Physocarpus opulifolius*), honeysuckle, Russian almond and double-flowering plum. If you spot broken, diseased, rubbing or winter-killed branches any time of year, however, prune them back to a suitable place below the problem area as soon as you can.

Bruce Peart says that at the Royal Botanical Gardens in Ontario, pruning is done soon after the flowers have faded. "We remove all the spent blooms, but in the back of our minds, we're always thinking about shape. We like to keep them short—short for a lilac, about 10 feet (3 m) tall—so that when people look at them, they're not craning their necks. We also cut out any crossing branches and broken or diseased branches. We're always shaping."

Don't trim shrubs with hedge shears to produce rounded heads. That sort of geometric pruning might work for cedar or yew, but it spoils the natural look of a lilac, removes flower buds and encourages branching at the top of the plant. Also, don't remove all the low branches and those that arch near the ground so that a mower can be run up to the base. The former removes all your new wood for potential flowering. The second practice destroys the natural shape of the shrub. Grass usually won't grow in such a shady place anyway, but if you do need to mow under the branches, raise them first. Alternatively, clear away the sod, and put down mulch or plant a low, shade-tolerant groundcover.

Remove new shoots (suckers) that grow from below the graft of grafted plants. Generally, the foliage will look different—probably smaller—than that of your desired variety. If you leave the suckers until they flower, you will have more than one type of flower on your plant, and the below-graft shoots may eventually dominate the shrub.

LILACS COMMON AND UNCOMMON

The previous pruning instructions apply to all lilacs. The following ones apply to the cultivars and hybrids of *S. vulgaris*—all the lilacs listed in Chapter 4, Lilacs Common and Uncommon. Pruning for shape and size probably won't be necessary during the lilac's first few years. Later, you may notice that the lower part of the shrub is becoming less floriferous and that there are tall, straight, thick branches. These are the branches that need to be thinned.

Frank Moro of Select Plus Nursery in Quebec says, "The rule of thumb is to remove one-quarter to one-third of the older wood every year, keeping the bulk of the bloom at eye level."

The cultivars and hybrids of *S. vulgaris* grow shoots from the base every year, gradually expanding their claim upon your garden. Unless these shoots are thinned, they can overrun perennial borders and strain relations with the neighbors. Some home gardeners remove all the suckers, the shoots that grow from the base of the shrub. The result is a tree-shaped shrub, not particularly floriferous, with one or a few older stems and flower buds that are high off the ground. Botanical gardens employ a different pruning method, because this year's suckers can be next year's flowering branches. After pruning, this method ideally leaves the shrub with a base of 9 to 15 stems of different ages.

Begin by standing back, looking at your shrub all

An Agriculture Canada drawing shows the ideal proportions of a lilac cutting whose lower leaves have been stripped off.

Preston lilacs such as 'Hiawatha,' ABOVE, *are less prone to suckering than* Syringa vulgaris *and its hybrids and cultivars.*

around and deciding what you will remove to improve its overall shape. Then follow these five steps:

1. With a pruning saw or small chainsaw, cut most of the oldest stems as close to the ground as you can, being careful not to harm the new shoots. An old branch can be tall and heavy, so you may need someone to hold it up as you saw. If your helper also pulls away from your sawing, your job will be much easier.

2. Cut other stems, including new suckers, to the ground, or dig them out entirely so that 9 to 15 shoots of various ages are left.

3. With pruning shears, cut out all dead, broken and rubbing branches, favoring those positioned to let in light and air.

4. Cut the newer shoots down by a third to a half, to a healthy branch union, as usual keeping in mind the overall shape and health of the plant.

5. Remove spent flowerheads from the remaining branches, cutting flush to the adjoining branch.

"Another trick of pruning," says Bruce Peart, "is knowing when to quit."

RENOVATING NEGLECTED LILACS

If you are renovating a plant that has been unpruned for years, you may be dealing with a small forest of suckers. Heavy pruning encourages more suckers to grow, so it is best to prune an overgrown lilac gradually. Take about three years to reach the ideal 9 to 15 shoots, doing a third of the pruning each year. The lilac may look somewhat unbalanced in the years it is undergoing renovation. You can renovate neglected shrubs in spring after bloom time, as in regular pruning, but if renovation is needed immediately, you may decide to go ahead

Some lilacs, including Syringa villosa, FACING PAGE, *are fairly easy to propagate from cuttings. Take healthy shoots,* LEFT, *trim off lower leaves,* CENTER, *dip bases in rooting hormone, plant upright, then enclose in a plastic bag,* RIGHT.

at a different time of year, knowing you will lose most of next year's flowers. Once the renovation is completed, continue with regular pruning every year.

If the shrub is in very poor shape, cut it back to a few inches above the ground. It should flower again in about two years. Severe pruning like this must not be done to a grafted lilac unless you are sure it has rooted from above the graft. If an old plant does not seem worth saving, you can always use whatever healthy growth you have to propagate a new plant by layering or taking cuttings (see above and pages 40-41).

No matter how heavily you prune, you need not use a tree-wound dressing. Many years of research by the U.S. Department of Agriculture showed that such dressings did not help the tree heal, nor did they keep out insects, prevent decay or control moisture flow. Provided your cuts are clean and the plant is healthy, nature will take care of healing the wounds.

MOVING A LILAC

Like all trees and shrubs, lilacs are easiest to move when young. The farther the roots have spread, the more damage you'll do when you dig it up and the heavier it will be. Unlike many trees and shrubs, however, lilacs take quite well to uprooting, especially the species and hybrids that tend to sucker. If you want to move a large plant, sever some of the roots several months before the move. With a sharp spade, draw a circle around the shrub as wide as the branch tips, or if this is too wide, make it as wide as the size of rootball you are able to lift. Divide the circle into six equal parts. In three alternating sections, cut straight down with the spade as far as it will go. When it is time to move the plant, dig down through the roots of the remaining three parts and pry up the rootball, cutting roots underneath the lilac as necessary. Growers of large lilac collections use a front-end loader, which can obtain a big enough root mass that roots need not be cut ahead of time. No matter how you move the lilac, water it deeply as soon as it is planted and then once a week for the remainder of the season, the same as for a newly purchased plant.

If you don't need the entire plant, you can simply remove rooted suckers. This is the best way to obtain wild, roadside or field plants, if they are what you want and if you have the permission of the landowner. (But if you grow a wildling, be prepared for biennial crops of relatively small flowers). For a nonsuckering species or cultivar, root layers or take cuttings.

WINTER PREPARATIONS

Hardy lilacs should not need protection in winter, although they should be sheltered from very strong winds. Only in places where winters are severe and snow cover is undependable is it wise to apply 4 inches (10 cm) of mulch around the base of each plant to protect the roots from frost damage. If you are in a place that has ice storms, you may want to tie the stems together loosely with twine.

In the south, you may need to withhold water to force the lilacs to drop their leaves, bringing on a partial dormancy. In his lilac garden in Leona Valley, California, Dr. Joel Margaretten waters his 300 to 500 plants until August 15, then waters only slightly if the weather is very hot. The rains start in November or December, encouraging the lilacs to bloom before Easter. Where there are no dependable winter rains, watering can be withheld from September through February.

MULTIPLICATION

If you want a copy of a favorite cultivar, try growing your own. The following four methods will give you a genetic copy, or clone, of the mother plant. Growing from seed gives you an entirely new individual.

Division: Plants that form suckers from the roots are the easiest to multiply. Wait until suckers are at least two years old before severing them from the parent plant, digging as deeply as possible to obtain roots.

Layering: This process encourages the plant to grow roots from a branch. Select a low-growing branch long enough to bend to the ground without breaking. Make a bare patch of soil where the branch contacts the ground. Scrape the bark at the contact point, dust the wound with rooting-hormone powder, and bend the branch to the ground, pinning the wound against the soil with a bent wire. Cover the contact point with about 4 inches (10 cm) of soil. Water the mound of soil, and weight the branch in place with a stone or brick. In two years, cut the branch connected to the mother plant, and transplant the new lilac.

Cuttings: Some lilacs are easy to multiply from softwood cuttings—the Prestons, the *hyacinthifloras* and 'Miss Kim,' for example. Some *S. vulgaris* cultivars are

Four-inch (10 cm) tissue-cultured lilacs for sale.

more difficult, but all are worth a try. Multiplying from cuttings is a faster process than layering, but the resulting plants are smaller. Take cuttings about two weeks after blooming has finished. For each one, remove about 6 inches (15 cm) of the tip of a healthy side branch, making the cut just below a leaf node with a sharp knife or secateurs. Cut the branch tip in the snappable softwood between the pliable growth at the branch tip and the hard growth from the previous year. Softwood cuttings are best taken in the early morning or on cloudy days. Remove all but the top few leaves from the cutting, and dip the base in water and then in rooting-hormone powder, available at plant nurseries.

Fill pots at least 4 inches (10 cm) deep with moist sterilized seedling mix. With a pencil or stick, make deep indentations in the mix, and insert a cutting in each hole. You can plant several cuttings in one con-

Hybrids and cultivars such as 'Krasavitsa Moskvy,' at left, ABOVE, *must be propagated vegetatively, not from seed.*

tainer, provided they are about 3 inches (7.5 cm) apart. A 6-inch (15-cm) plastic flowerpot, for instance, could hold about four evenly spaced cuttings. Water the soil. Enclose the pot and the cuttings in a clear plastic bag, close the top with a twist tie, and place the bag in a spot outdoors that is shaded all day. Lilacs generally take two to six weeks to root, although there will be some failures. When roots grow out of the holes in the base of the pot or the cutting feels firm when you tug it gently, remove the plastic bag. Keep the soil watered and the pot in shade for a week, then move it into partial sun.

Don't leave the cuttings in pots over the winter in areas colder than zone 6. Instead, overwinter them in nursery beds or directly where they will grow. Mulch them deeply, as they are not as hardy as they will be later. Water them regularly in dry weather, not only right away but also the next spring and summer.

Grafting: A short length of lilac branch tip, the scion, is joined with a rooted stem, the stock, which can be another type of lilac or else privet or ash, both of which are close relatives of lilac. Many books describe grafting in detail.

Tissue culture or micropropagation: These cloning techniques, in which small amounts of tissue are grown under controlled conditions, are used by commercial greenhouses to create many new plants in a relatively small amount of space.

Seeds: Growing a lilac from seed may result in a plant that is quite different from the parent in color and other characteristics, so it is an age-old propagation method for lilac breeders. If you are patient, growing lilacs from seed can be fun. Your chances of creating an improved cultivar will be best if you choose two superior parents and artificially pollinate the flower of one with the pollen of a flower from the other, then ensure that no more pollen reaches the female parent, not even its own pollen. Some lilacs, such as 'Lavender Lady,' 'Mme Lemoine' and 'Rochester' have been especially popular parents. Lilac breeder John Fiala writes that he removed the female parent's petals before it opened, then dusted the pistil with the desired pollen and covered the flower with a small bag for a day or so to prevent further pollination. The bag was then removed to allow the seeds to develop normally.

Lilac seeds require stratification—a period of cold and moisture—before they will germinate. Nature's way is the easiest. Lightly cover the seeds on fertile weeded soil in fall, and let winter do its work. The seeds should germinate when the soil warms in spring. Sprouting should take about 10 days for most species, although some seeds can take as long as six weeks. Seedlings may grow 6 to 8 inches tall (15-20 cm) the first year. Indoors, the seeds can be sown in pots on the surface of moist seedling mixture. Place the pots in tied plastic bags or covered containers in a refrigerator for three weeks. Then move the pots to a warm spot— 70 degrees F (21°C). When spring frosts have ended, move the pots outdoors to a place with partial shade that is protected from strong winds. Water daily. When the seedlings have several leaves, plant them in shaded beds. The following year, they can be moved to a sunny bed. It generally takes four to six years for *S. vulgaris* seedlings to reach flowering size.

STANDARDS

A standard is a woody plant grafted to the top of a single straight stem, resulting in a topknot appearance. The usual stem for lilacs was once privet, but these grafts are susceptible to disease. Dave Bakker, Sr., retired propagation manager of J.C. Bakker & Sons, one of the nurseries that sells lilac standards wholesale, explained that after trials with several types of stock, including *S. vulgaris* (too many suckers), *S. reticulata* subsp. *reticulata* (often incompatible with the scion) and *S. reticulata* subsp. *pekinensis* (not very straight), they settled upon the Hungarian lilac (*S. josikaea*). This species is hardy, seldom suckers, grows easily from softwood cuttings and relatively quickly produces a straight stem the required 6 to 8 feet tall (1.8-2.5 m). If suckers develop after grafting, their foliage is sufficiently different from the grafted variety that a home gardener can tell the difference and prune the suckers away. Many cultivars are now available on standards. Among those sold by Hortico Inc. are 'Charles Joly,' 'Lavender Lady,' 'Miss Ellen Willmott' and 'Mrs. Harry Bickle.' "Anywhere you can grow a lilac, you can grow a standard," says Dave Bakker.

An adventurous gardener wishing to create a standard should grow a stem from a cutting to create the stock, then using the traditional techniques outlined in any book on grafting, cut off the top of the stock and graft to it the scion, the desired cultivar.

Incidentally, for those who enjoy grafting, an old book provides another challenge. Writing about *S. vulgaris* in *The New American Gardener* in 1843,

A treelike standard results from grafting a lilac to a straight stem. The Lemoine hybrid 'Prodige,' FACING PAGE, is a candidate, while 'Primrose,' ABOVE, has been grafted.

Thomas G. Fessenden said, "The white and the purple may be easily grafted, or inoculated, into each other, and when the shrub, with a handsome head is thus managed, some branches producing purple and others white flowers, it makes a beautiful appearance."

FORCING LILACS

Forced lilacs for the Christmas market are to western Europe what poinsettias are to the United States and Canada.

In commercial forcing, lilac shoots grafted densely on rootstocks are stored in greenhouses where the temperature and atmosphere can be adjusted to a schedule that initiates flowering in early December. At home, the easiest way to force lilacs is to pick budded branches in early spring and bring them indoors to a cool place to bloom. You won't have lilacs for Christmas, but you'll have them ahead of outdoors. 'Palibin' is one of the easiest lilacs to force at home.

Into the Garden

Lilacs in the landscape

"IN THE DOORYARD FRONTING AN OLD FARM-HOUSE NEAR THE WHITE-WASH'D PALINGS,
STANDS THE LILAC-BUSH TALL-GROWING WITH HEART-SHAPED LEAVES OF RICH GREEN,
WITH MANY A POINTED BLOSSOM RISING DELICATE, WITH THE PERFUME STRONG I LOVE,
WITH EVERY LEAF A MIRACLE—AND FROM THIS BUSH IN THE DOORYARD,
WITH DELICATE-COLOR'D BLOSSOM AND HEART-SHAPED LEAVES OF RICH GREEN,
A SPRIG WITH ITS FLOWER I BREAK."

—Walt Whitman, "When Lilacs Last in the Dooryard Bloom'd" (1865)

At the Hulda Klager Lilac Garden in the state of Washington, there are lilacs "tall-growing," much as Whitman's must have been. Near a white fence that fronts the old Klager house is a purple-flowering lilac that Klager developed and named for her husband, Frank, who died long before her.

Plant a lilac, and you plant a memory. Whitman's poem, a tribute to a beloved statesman, was originally entitled "Memories of President Lincoln." A lilac, more than any other shrub, will lend your landscape the aura of nostalgia, the remembrance of springs and summers past. The sweetness of lilac perfume, most precious in places where winters are harshest, comes at a time of year when the renewal of life is still apt to be interrupted by frost, when every leaf is, as Whitman writes, a miracle. Certainly the common lilac, with its heady promise that summer is around the corner, rivals only the rose in

its hold on our emotions. The species lilacs contribute entirely different garden elements: beauty, yes, but predominantly the surprise that these plants are lilacs at all.

Syringa vulgaris 'Frank' was in full flower when I visited the Klager garden in early May. Klager herself died in 1960, leaving her garden in the devoted care of volunteers. Just inside the front gate, 'Frank' was one of the taller elements in a perennial border of phlox, azaleas and rhododendrons, with ajuga and campanula as groundcovers. The Klager garden is that rare and lovely marriage for a lilac lover—a well-tended home garden, but one in which the lilacs are labeled.

LOCATION

In most gardens, a lilac will be just one of a range of shrubs in a varied collection of trees, perennials and annuals planted in accordance with lawns and build-

Landscape plans combine lilacs with contemporaries such as poppies and salvia as well as other plants that will bloom later.

Among horticulturist Hulda Klager's releases are white 'Chrystal' and magenta 'Frank,' named for her husband.

ings. When you purchase a lilac, you probably already have an idea of where you want it to go. Place may even take precedence over variety, as in "We need something to fill that empty space by the deck. How about a lilac?" On the other hand, maybe you want to find the perfect spot for a favorite lilac. In either case, take some time to make sure you have the best position for your lilac and the best neighbors for it if there will be other plants nearby.

Give your lilac plenty of space. Most shrubby lilacs mature at about 12 feet (3.7 m) tall and almost as wide, although many grow taller, while dwarfs such as 'Miss Kim,' 'Palibin' and 'Prairie Petite' may stay half that size. If you are inclined to prune, you can keep your shrub much smaller. Tree lilacs, which should be left unpruned except for dead flowers and dead or damaged wood, can eventually reach about 25 feet (7.6 m).

First, a reminder from the previous chapter: Whatever position a lilac takes in the landscape, it needs as much sun as possible in zones 2 to 6, but in warmer gardens, it will do best with at least an hour of midday shade. And it needs well-drained soil.

Forget the concept of "foundation planting," as it was called. A century ago, a landscaping axiom had it that shrubs and small trees, both evergreen and deciduous, planted right next to the house would cover the foundation and visually connect the house to the landscape when seen by passersby. The problem was that while foundation plantings may have made the house look better for a while, not only could they scarcely be seen from indoors but they rapidly outgrew their roles, blocking windows, rubbing against walls and stretching past the roofline. The new advice is to plant shrubs and trees where they can be seen from in-

In the Klager garden, a modestly flowering 'Pink Elizabeth' lilac is not upstaged by a showy rhododendron behind.

doors or from vantage points outdoors such as your lawn or deck. When seen from the sidewalk or road, such plantings still beautify the landscape.

A lilac that will be 8 feet (2.5 m) wide in three or four years—as most of them will—should not be planted an arm's length from a wall, the neighbor's fence or another shrub or tree. Six feet (1.8 m) may feel like a mile when you plant your twiggy little purchase, but it is a safe minimum distance unless you've bought a dwarf. Remember that other trees and shrubs near your lilac are also going to grow bigger. Until they do, you can fill the spaces between with annuals or perennials. Look up, too—don't plant your lilac directly under a clothesline, tree branches or a telephone wire unless they are higher than the eventual height of your lilac. You don't want to have to move

or remove your lilac in a couple of years, or five or ten, by which time it will be huge and heavy. Situate it well at the outset, and save yourself headaches in years to come. Put a shovel upright in the ground where you think your lilac might go and walk around it to see how it looks, imagining its mature height and width and its appeal both in and out of bloom.

THREE ROLES

At the Hulda Klager garden, lilacs are grown in three main landscape roles: on their own as specimen plants; in groupings of shrubs, either formal or informal; and in beds of perennials.

The lilac as specimen—that is, planted on its own as a focal point—is the most common way of planting. At the Klager garden, for example, one 'Alice Eastwood' shrub is as graceful as a swan in its pond of mulched soil. Elsewhere, the lilac-blue flowers of a lone 'President Lincoln' are given the backdrop, several yards away, of the white flowers of *Viburnum plicatum tomentosum* in full bloom. Leave enough space all around a specimen that it can extend to a proportional width and can be seen from all angles, presenting different backgrounds from each vantage point. Suckers can be easily spotted and removed, and those that venture as far as the lawn can be mowed. The downside of specimen planting is that when the lilac has finished blooming, its spot in the garden is less interesting.

A lilac in a shrub border is an extension of the specimen idea. Again the shrubs are set apart from annuals and perennials, but here, one shrub may pick up the limelight when another finishes blooming. At the Klager garden, a long bed mulched with wood chips is home to three shrubs—the lilacs 'Pink Elizabeth' and white 'Glory' to the right and left of a rose of Sharon (*Hibiscus syriacus*), which begins to leaf out as the lilacs bloom and flowers as they fade. There are many possible substitutes for the rose of Sharon, including any of the companion shrubs listed later in this chapter. This bed of three shrubs, all 10 to 12 feet (3-3.7 m) tall and 6 feet (1.8 m) apart, is surrounded by lawn that separates the trio from a fence on one side and a perennial border on the other. Looking beyond the shrubs toward the perennial border in early

May, one can see skimmia, azaleas, irises and daylilies yet to bloom and a 'King George' rhododendron in fabulous flower. Planted under the lilacs, the king would have commanded all the attention, but the distance between the lilac and perennial beds gives both species space to shine (see photograph on page 47).

A large bed of shrubs hardy to zone 3, designed for a 1944 Agriculture Canada booklet, includes a lilac and a flowering crab as the tallest elements flanking three honeysuckles. In front of these five tall background plants grow three pink-flowered weigelas, two white-flowered hydrangeas and three white-flowered mock oranges (*Philadelphus*). This bed would be very easy to maintain and remain attractive all season.

Another landscape position for a lilac is in a perennial border, provided the lilac is not such an exuberant producer of shoots that it will threaten to overwhelm its neighbors. Many a lovely bed of perennials has been overrun by *S. vulgaris* on a rampage. Be diligent with annual pruning (see the previous chapter), or let suckering lilacs grow as specimens or with other shrubs, where their suckers can be easily seen and dealt with.

GROUNDCOVERS

Growing a lilac within a perennial border means that something living will have to grow under the shrub. A dense perennial groundcover that keeps weeds out will mean less digging close to the lilac, where its shallow roots might otherwise be damaged. The best groundcover choices are low and drought-tolerant. Any of the spreading cranesbills (*Geranium* spp.) are beautiful, as are snow-in-summer (*Cerastium tomentosum*) and periwinkle (*Vinca minor*)—both determined colonizers best allowed to fill a small bed surrounded by lawn. Consider also forget-me-not (*Myosotis*), aubrieta, speedwell (*Veronica repens*) and any of the hostas. Lime-green and variegated leaves are especially showy under dark green lilac foliage.

At Van Dusen Gardens in Vancouver, the pale yellow *S. vulgaris* 'Primrose' and smaller *S. meyeri* 'Palibin' grow beside a tall black locust (*Robinia pseudoacacia*) in a bed of shrubs and perennials. In early May, 'Palibin' blooms in synchrony with campanulas, cranesbills and *Hydrangea macrophylla* 'Mowe.' *Hydrangea serrata* 'Preziosa' has finished blooming. The

Growing Syringa vulgaris *as a specimen,* FACING PAGE, *gives it sun and allows suckers to be easily pruned or mowed.*

LILACS WITH INTERESTING FOLIAGE

Note that because lilacs with variegated foliage lack a full complement of chlorophyll, they can be slower-growing and more difficult than their green-leafed counterparts. Gold-leafed plants should be given full sun. They turn greener as the season progresses. Leaves that are dappled or variegated with white should have some shade.

- ❧ *S.* x *diversifolia*, a hybrid of *S. protolaciniata* and *S. pinnatifolia*: pinnate, entire, intermediate leaves; gold in fall
- ❧ *S. emodi* 'Aurea': gold foliage
- ❧ *S.* x *hyacinthiflora* 'Corinna's Mist': speckled leaves that turn burgundy in fall
- ❧ *S.* x *laciniata*: cut leaves
- ❧ *S. pinnatifolia*: compound leaves
- ❧ *S. protolaciniata*: fernlike foliage

- ❧ *S. reticulata* subsp. *amurensis* 'Chantilly Lace': yellow-green variegated leaves that turn creamy yellow in summer
- ❧ *S. reticulata* subsp. *reticulata*
  'Cameo's Jewel': mottled green-and-yellow foliage
  'China Gold': gold-to-pale-green foliage
  'Golden Eclipse': variegated green-and-white foliage
- ❧ *S. tomentella* 'Kum-Bum': golden foliage
- ❧ *S. villosa* 'Aurea': golden foliage
- ❧ *S. vulgaris*
  'Aucubaefolia': gold-and-green variegated foliage and single bluish flowers
  'Dappled Dawn': dappled leaves and single bluish flowers.

'Primrose' lilac, tree peonies and columbines (*Aquilegia*) are yet to bloom.

At the Hulda Klager garden, extensive use is made of the groundcovers campanula, phlox, daylily and, in the shadier areas, epimedium. Watch out for fragrant groundcovers such as lily-of-the-valley and sweet woodruff, whose scent might compete with that of lilacs.

The height of the groundcover under the lilacs will depend upon how bare you keep the lilac stems. In any case, beyond the edge of the lilac branches, taller perennials can grow. This is a favorite position for hardy bulbs such as tulips, narcissus and alliums, many of which bloom at the same time as the lilac, so if carefully chosen for color, they can present breathtaking garden pictures. Hardy bulbs are drought-tolerant, another advantage, because lilacs tend to take moisture out of the surrounding soil. Additional perennial companions include tall artemisias such as 'Silver King' and 'Valerie Finnis,' coral bells (*Heuchera*), lamb's ears (*Stachys lanata*), perennial salvia (*Salvia nemorosa* and *S.* x *superba*), peonies, yarrow (*Achillea* spp. and cultivars) and ornamental grasses. *Miscanthus sinensis* and its many cultivars suit taller lilacs, whereas the small *Festuca glauca* and *Pennisetum alopecuroides* 'Hameln' suit dwarf lilacs such as 'Minuet,' 'Miss Kim,' 'Miss Canada' and 'Palibin.'

SCENE STEALERS

Although parts of the Klager garden remain much as Hulda planted them, other parts have changed with the years. Western Washington state is ideal camellia, rhododendron and azalea country, so these shrubs and small trees feature large and bright at lilac time. When grown too close to the rather subtle and small-flowered lilacs, they steal the show.

These shrubs are not the only potential scene stealers at lilac time, especially in gardens warmer than climatic zone 5. Any large- or bright-flowered spring shrub or tree such as dogwood, magnolia or Japanese flowering cherry can eclipse a lilac that's planted too close. Neighboring flower size matters, but so does color: Watch out for the brilliant pinks that some azaleas flaunt but lilacs cannot match and the reds of flowering quinces and some crabapples, maples and camellias. Only a white lilac will look harmonious next to red, but it, too, can be reduced

Single white lilacs, described as SI by fanciers, come into their own late in the day. This is Syringa *x* persica *'Alba.'*

from starlet to understudy by bigger flowers growing at the same height. Lilacs are too polite to fight for center stage during their brief season of bloom.

TREE LILACS

Tree lilacs can take a place in a perennial or shrub border, but they can also hold more commanding positions in the landscape. Because they grow taller than the shrubs, to about 20 to 25 feet (6-7.5 m), they are less easily outdone by bright-blooming shrubs of other species. They can be used to shade a deck or the sunny side of a house. The most common of the tree lilacs at the time of publication is 'Ivory Silk,' which is winning praise throughout the northern states and southern Canada as an excellent candidate for roadsides and home gardens. It is disease- and pollution-tolerant, puts up with poor, dry and even

Tree lilacs, or standards, are tall enough to make a strong visual statement, no matter what else is in bloom in the vicinity.

salty soil, blooms in summer, does not sucker, has good fall color and forms a neat upright shape. Plant a row close to a sidewalk, or feature a single tree in a sunny spot surrounded by lawn. The arching habits of S. *reticulata* and its subspecies make them especially suited to Japanese-style gardens. In addition, some of the taller shrub lilacs, especially the Prestons, can be pruned to three to five stems and grown as small trees that reach about 12 feet (7.5 m) in height.

COLOR

Although there are hundreds of subtle color differences in lilacs, *Syringa* scientists and fanciers have reduced the palette to seven numbers. You may encounter this system in a catalog or at a nursery:

I White
II Violet
III Bluish
IV Lilac
V Pinkish
VI Magenta
VII Purple

Bicolors have combined numbers. For example, a purple-and-white lilac such as 'Sensation' is labeled VII & I. Numbers are joined for color blends. Thus the purplish violet 'Vesper' is VII/II or VII-II, and the violet-purple 'Flower City' is II/VII or II-VII. Singles are marked S, and doubles D.

How your lilac's flower color will fit your landscape is a very personal matter. You may grow several varieties close together with similar colors, say purples and magentas, or perhaps a palette of lilac shades, since all harmonize. Or you may grow just one lilac in your favorite color. There are no truly red, orange or bright

True pink and true blue lilacs are rare; even the optimistically named 'True Blue' is tinted lilac.

yellow lilacs, although there are magentas and one lone pale yellow—'Primrose.' Lilac colors can change somewhat from season to season, certainly from garden to garden, depending on soil conditions and weather. They are brighter in cool, damp seasons than they are in hot, sunny, dry ones.

Consider what color will look best against your house walls and next to your other plants and what will please you most when you cut the flowers and bring them indoors. The flowers of the darkest inky purple lilacs such as 'Mrs. W.E. Marshall' tend to disappear into the shadows of the foliage, while the whites shine brightest. John Fiala writes, "A special kind of unity in the garden is obtained with white lilacs, a kind of fragrant freshness, a sense of restful completeness and of quiet propriety." White is the best color for late in the day, and whites are often fragrant, so if you like to spend early-summer

evenings on the deck or in the garden, consider white.

On the other hand, there are plenty of other spring-flowering shrubs with white flowers, whereas lilacs are best known not only for the color lilac—actually one of the rarer colors amongst the cultivated varieties—but also for every shade from pink to dark purple. Pale pinks fade into rosy hues, into pink and dark magentas, into purples from lavender to violet to indigo. The best companion plants will have flower colors that are complementary or fall within the lilac spectrum. In their garden of about 90 lilacs in Alfred, Maine, Howard and Carolyn Merrill grow pink, white and lilac tulips. "If there's a red tulip," says Carolyn, "it's a mistake."

Pinks are among the most fragile of lilac colors—and the most coveted, especially the early 'Maiden's Blush' followed by 'Lucie Baltet.' Pinks can turn warmer or cooler with the acidity or alkalinity of the soil and are

'Esther Staley' is brightened by a shady background.

apt to fade quickly in bright sun. The pink lilacs enjoy a bit of shade. Russian lilac breeder Kolesnikov cautioned that pink, lilac and blue lilacs should be planted in soil that is about neutral in pH for best color. Blues tend toward pinkish, even the lovely 'True Blue,' but the best and truest of the blues are to my eyes those developed by John Fiala, such as 'Wedgwood Blue' and 'Wonderblue.' You'll find it helpful if you can see a variety of labeled lilacs in bloom at a botanical or private garden.

BLOOM TIME

Each lilac will bloom for about two weeks, from the opening of the first bud to the fading of the last flowers, although hot spring weather will shorten bloom time. If you have a sufficiently large garden, you can have six weeks of lilac flowers by planting several species with overlapping bloom times. The following

schedule is generally about right for zones 4 to 6. The same early-through-very-late flowering sequence will occur elsewhere, but the dates will differ.

Early (early May):
S. x hyacinthiflora, S. oblata, S. pinnatifolia,
S. vulgaris 'Rhodopea'
Midseason (mid-May):
S. x chinensis, S. meyeri, S. x persica, S. pubescens,
S. vulgaris
Late (late May to early June):
S. emodi, S. x henryi, S. x josiflexa, S. komarowii,
S. x nanceiana, S. x prestoniae, S. reflexa,
S. sweginzowii, S. tomentella, S. wolfii, S. yunnanensis
Very late (June):
S. reticulata

In addition, *S. meyeri* and *S. pubescens* subsp. *microphylla* may bloom again in fall.

GARDEN COMPANIONS

Since an individual lilac blooms for a fairly short time, the landscape should include annuals, perennials and shrubs that bloom earlier or later. Consistent color in the lilac bed can come from bedding annuals that flower until fall frost.

Colorful foliage can also attract attention all season. Most lilacs have dark green foliage that is an excellent foil for shrubs with golden, purple or variegated foliage. Among the gold-leafed shrubs, consider euphorbia, ninebark (*Physocarpus opulifolius*), golden mock orange (*Philadelphus coronarius aureus*), *Caryopteris* 'Worcester Gold' or one of the golden forms of elder (*Sambucus nigra*). Purple-leafed shrubs include smoke tree (*Cotinus coggygria*) 'Royal Purple,' sand cherry (*Prunus x cistena*), sumac (*Rhus typhina*)—but prune out suckers—'Royalty' crabapple and *Physocarpus opulifolius* Diabolo®. Variegated shrubs include cultivars of weigela and dogwood. Consider any of the evergreen cultivars of white cedar, arborvitae or juniper as companions that provide year-round color. Taller conifers of any species look wonderful as a backdrop on the northern side of lilacs.

Training a clematis to climb into a lilac gives the shrub a longer season of interest, although it may make pruning difficult. Some clematis vines will inevitably fall victim to the secateurs unless you are an infrequent or very careful pruner. The small-flowered species such as *Clematis montana* and sweet autumn clematis (*C. paniculata*) are especially eager to clamber, although even the large-flowered hybrids will make their way upward, creating the illusion of a clematis shrub in June or July.

LILACS IN CONTAINERS

Lilacs in containers are suited to the smallest gardens and to rooftops, decks and balconies. The smallest container lilacs are bonsai. Kyosuke Gun of Japan created a blooming *S. vulgaris* about 4 inches (10 cm) tall with tiny fragrant flowers in a dish small enough to fit on the palm of his hand. This sort of miniature creation is the work of the artist.

Choose a dwarf or small lilac for your container. The best container varieties include *S. meyeri*, *S. oblata* subsp. *dilatata*, *S. patula*, *S. pubescens* and dwarf forms of *S. vulgaris* such as purple 'Minuet,' pink-magenta 'Little Miss Muffet,' bluish 'Munchkin,' single white 'Pixie' and purple 'Prairie Petite' and 'Purple Gem,' all singles. Also, look at the list of interspecific hybrids on pages 95-96, many of which are dwarfs. The dwarf lilacs are as floriferous as their larger cousins, and some are fragrant. One of the most fragrant, *S. pubescens* subsp. *microphylla* will grow well in a cool greenhouse, where it flowers about six weeks earlier than it would outdoors.

Use a strong, attractive container that has drainage holes. The larger the container, the better insulated from extremes of heat and cold the roots will be, the less danger there will be of roots overheating or freezing, and the less often you'll have to water. Stay away from black plastic, which absorbs so much heat that roots could burn. Situate your pot before filling, plant-

The foliage of 'Aucubaefolia' is as attractive as its flowers.

ing and watering it, as it will be heavy afterward. Place the container where it will receive at least six hours of sun a day, use good topsoil, and remember to water whenever the soil is dry an inch (2.5 cm) below the surface. Don't water until the surface dries out, as the dwarfs are especially intolerant of constant wetness.

In zone 6 or warmer, lilacs in containers can be left outdoors year-round, but where winters are more se-

LILACS WITH GOOD FALL COLOR

ɔ჻ *S. x hyacinthiflora*: turns burgundy

ɔ჻ *S. meyeri* and 'Palibin': turn dark maroon

ɔ჻ *S. oblata* and 'Cheyenne': turn bronze to dark purple

ɔ჻ *S. pubescens* subsp. *patula* and cultivars: turn burgundy

ɔ჻ *S. vulgaris*: some white-flowered forms turn yellow.

A mixed hedge in Vancouver, Canada, successfully partners an informal lilac with pruned pieris and English laurel.

vere, the roots may be damaged by the cold. Either remove the lilac from the container and heel it into the garden for the winter or bury the lilac container in soil, leaves or straw. Don't bring the lilac indoors, because the flower buds need cold to mature.

HEDGING BETS

Lilacs can form all or part of a hedge to define the edge of your property or an area within the landscape. The hedge might be made up of one type of lilac or several, or it could be a mixture of shrub species, be they deciduous, broadleaf evergreens or conifers, provided the hedgemates will tolerate pruning and grow to about the same height and width as the lilac. I grow lilacs in a hedge that includes highbush cranberry (*Viburnum trilobum*) and variegated European elder (*Sambucus nigra*). Other suitable hedgemates include bridalwreath spiraea (*Spiraea* x van-

houttei), ninebark (*Physocarpus opulifolius*), mock orange (*Philadelphus* spp.), white cedar (*Thuja occidentalis*), upright rather than spreading forms of juniper and, in zone 6 or warmer, English laurel (*Prunus laurocerasus*). The best lilacs for hedges are medium-sized, dense, hardy and resistant to pests and diseases.

S. x *chinensis* flowers abundantly and is almost maintenance-free; a good medium-sized hedge.

S. *josikaea* makes a good taller hedge but requires better soil than does S. x *chinensis*. It looks best if pruned to about 5 feet (1.5 m). Left unpruned, it can reach 15 feet (4.5 m).

S. *meyeri* 'Palibin' makes a very good small- to medium-sized hedge. It is resistant to powdery mildew, stays dense without much pruning and blooms heavily in spring and sometimes again in late summer. In 1986, it was named one of the favorite 10 hedge plants

Syringa x chinensis *is one of the species recommended for use on its own as an easy medium-sized hedge.*

by employees of the Horticulture Department of Daws Arboretum near Columbus, Ohio. It is also the top hedging choice of Charles Holetich, retired curator of the lilac collection at the Royal Botanical Gardens.

S. x *persica* forms a medium-sized, disease- and pest-resistant hedge 6 to 8 feet (1.8- 2.5 m) tall that produces pale lilac flowers in spring. It survives dry wind.

S. *pubescens* subsp. *patula* 'Miss Kim' makes a good low hedge 3 to 6 feet (0.9-1.8 m) tall. It is disease- and pest-resistant, has annual bloom and fall color.

S. *reticulata* subsp. *amurensis* makes a good tall hedge when allowed to grow several stems. At the Agriculture Canada research station in Morden, Manitoba, it grew into a hedge 9 feet (2.7 m) high and 4 feet (1.2 m) wide. There, it was trimmed carefully with pruners or a knife so that the handsome leaves would not be mutilated.

S. *vulgaris* has been planted as a hedge throughout the Canadian prairies. At the Agriculture Canada research station in Morden, Manitoba, this hedge is clipped once a year in late June. Set out in 1931, the hedge grew to 10 feet (3 m) high and 5 feet (1.5 m) wide at the base, but in October 1960, it was trimmed back to 3 feet (0.9 m) high and 18 inches (45 cm) wide at the base and maintained at that size. It was recommended that common lilac be ruthlessly desuckered to keep it within bounds. Sever the shoots fairly close to the center of the hedge, but keep in mind the recommended ideal dimensions.

PLANTING A HEDGE

The Agriculture Canada booklet "Hedges for the Prairies" (Harp and Cumming, revised 1974), based on 40 years of testing hedge plants at the Agriculture Canada research station in Morden, Manitoba, instructs that for a medium-height deciduous hedge, plants should be spaced 18 inches (45 cm) apart in a single straight row.

Cut the plants back after planting to develop bushy shrubs with low, twiggy branches. Unless you prune the stock properly at planting time, the shrubs will be leggy and you will never have a satisfactory hedge. The shape that best combines beauty with utility is sometimes called the "inverted vee" or "narrow pyramid," 3 feet (0.9 m) wide at the ground and 5 feet (1.5 m) high. The top should be slightly rounded and no wider than a foot (30 cm). A hedge like this is easier to trim, and it remains alive and bushy right to its base because all of it is exposed to the sun.

After the first pruning is done at planting time, you need do nothing more except weed until the following spring. Then, using a string to keep the work straight, cut all the old wood to the base, and reduce the remaining shoots to two-thirds of their length, pruning to a point where the new growth is developing. You may also need to cut out some younger wood to maintain a well-shaped hedge.

FRAGRANCE

I like to think that the lilac's genus name *Syringa* pays homage, in a roundabout way, to fragrance. The genus is named after Syrinx, a nymph of Greek legend who was transformed into a hollow reed. That reed was used to make the pipes of Pan, so Syrinx lived on invisibly in the shepherd god's music. The lilac's perfume is just as haunting, invisible and airborne as Syrinx.

More prosaically, plant perfume isn't the stuff of legends at all but mere molecules of volatile compounds sent out as invitations to flying pollinators. Cold weather inhibits plant fragrances; hot weather burns them off quickly. Warm, sunny, somewhat dry mornings and evenings, when pollinators fly best, are the times when these irresistible flirtations are most noticeable. It's simply our good luck that we humans share the insects' olfactory preferences.

Perfume molecules come into contact with nerves behind the bridge of our nose. Thus begins a short circuit to the brain and the emotions. A part of our brain so primitive that it allowed our ancestors to survive by sniffing out danger, food and sex makes the decision: pleasant, indifferent, unpleasant. Smell is the oldest of the five senses and is linked with the basic behaviors of approach and avoidance, the foundations of emotion.

In 1986, the staff at the Smell and Taste Center at the University of Pennsylvania helped create a test published in *Omni* magazine. Readers were asked to report their response to various scratch-and-sniff fragrances. The majority of some 20,000 readers gave the top votes to flowers, including lilacs.

Common opinion has it that the best lilac fragrance comes from the wild shrub of the roadsides and romance, *S. vulgaris*. While fields of wild lilacs can be almost overpowering in late May, the species *vulgaris*, when put to the test, has not emerged as sweetest of all. It rated only average in recent trials at the Arnold Arboretum, when plant propagator John Alexander III, admittedly "not very sensitive to fragrance," enlisted two people to accompany him through the lilac collection. They rated the lilacs from 0 (no fragrance) to 3 (maximum fragrance). From 195 plants sampled in 1982, they ended up with a mean rating of 0.78. From 261 plants sniffed in 1983, the mean was 1.3, an increase that Alexander could only suppose might, "like the taste of wine," indicate the changeability of lilac fragrance or of one's sensitivity to it.

Over the two years, the fragrance of the wild *S. vulgaris* rated 0.75, a little less than the mean. The only *S. vulgaris* cultivars rated above 2 were 'Evangeline,' 'Henri Martin,' 'Pascal' and the highest, 'Serene,' with a top rating of 3. But also rated at 3 were a group of lesser-known hybrids and species: *S. x chinensis* 'Metensis' and 'Saugeana,' *S. oblata* subsp. *oblata*, *S. pubescens* subsp. *pubescens* and *S. pubescens* subsp. *julianae*. Others judge the heirloom lilac-colored single *S. vulgaris* 'Marlyensis' to be one of the most fragrant.

But of course, one person's sweet may be another's *poisson*. While some lilacs are considered pleasant by almost everybody and some are considered unpleasant by almost everybody—the latter including the tree lilacs and *S. villosa*, which even lilac enthusiast Alice Harding judged "rather unpleasant"—there is little common ground. Harding decided she couldn't choose a favorite lilac on the basis of fragrance. "There is not one without which I would willingly live."

The unpleasant-smelling lilacs are sometimes described as "spicy," while those with scents most people find haunting and beautiful may repel or induce allergic reactions in others. In her award-winning novel

The Good House, Bonnie Burnard refers to "the stink of lilacs." Indoors, I find the fragrance claustrophobic. So did John Gerard, who wrote about lilacs in his famous herbal of the early 17th century: "I once gathered the floures and layed them in my chamber window, which smelled more strongly after they had lien together a few hourse, with such an unacquainted savor that they awaked me out of sleepe, so that I could not rest till I had cast them out of my chamber."

I think lilacs smell best outdoors. A little like the music of Syrinx, the pipes of Pan.

LILACS INDOORS

Lilacs of all types are fabulous as cut flowers. Their woody stems support them at different angles, so even a bunch set casually in a bucket of water becomes a work of art. Their tiny flowers are already in bunches, and the scent of many is intoxicating.

Cut lilacs in the morning while the air is still cool. For the longest show, cut them when they are partially, not fully, open. Cut branches long enough to display them well in their containers, but pay attention to the shape and balance of the shrub or tree, even if the lilacs are wild.

Dr. Owen Rogers of the University of New Hampshire found that lilacs lasted longest if he took a pail of warm water into the field where he was cutting. Lukewarm water moves into the stem faster than cold. Leave the lilacs in the warm water for at least 20 minutes before arranging them in cool water. Better yet, leave the flowers in warm water at least two hours or even overnight. This process, called conditioning, is used by florists both amateur and professional to prepare flowers for shows and competitions.

Before you arrange lilacs (or any cut flower), wash the vase with a fresh solution of 10 parts water to 1 part household bleach to kill bacteria that could multiply and clog the stems. Rinse the vase, then fill with cool water. Use rainwater or distilled water if possible,

because water high in fluoride, chlorine or salts speeds the death of cut flowers. Add a commercial flower preservative, or substitute a small amount of light-colored soft drink—not diet drink.

Rogers found that hammering the base of the stem, which is sometimes advised, made no difference in how long the cut lilacs lasted. What did make a difference was stripping off all the lower leaves that might otherwise be underwater. Removing this foliage at cutting time added a day to the life of the cut flowers.

Recut the branches underwater using a sharp knife held at an angle. Rogers writes, "I cut some lilacs at home and placed them promptly in plain water. In two days, they began to wilt but quickly recovered when I recut the stems underwater. Apparently if you catch the initial wilting, it can be corrected."

Lilacs can be arranged alone or with other shrubs, flowers, grasses or foliage. Harmonious colors of tulips look fabulous. Use only freshly cut material. Avoid daffodils (*Narcissus*) because they exude a substance that shortens the life of other cut flowers. If you are using florist's foam, or oasis, use only fresh foam, because it can harbor bacteria that shorten the life of the flowers. Keep the arrangement in a cool place away from sunny windows, hot air vents and televisions. Lilacs will last longest—about 11 days—at 35 to 41 degrees F (2-5°C).

A single lilac branch makes an instant bouquet. It will last longest if cut before all the florets are open.

Lilacs Common and Uncommon

Syringa vulgaris, its hybrids and cultivars

"SOME DECLARE THAT THERE ARE TOO MANY NAMED SORTS OF THE COMMON LILAC AND THAT THE DIFFERENCES ARE OFTEN SO SLIGHT AS TO BE ALMOST ABSENT....BUT TO THE RANK AND FILE, THE ABUNDANCE OF BLOSSOMS IS A JOY SO GREAT THAT CRITICISM CANNOT FOR AN INSTANCE LIVE IN OUR THOUGHTS."

—E.H. Wilson, *America's Greatest Garden, The Arnold Arboretum* (1925)

Many a passionate lilac lover maintains that nothing but the common lilac, *Syringa vulgaris*, is really a lilac. Other species are imposters, *Syringa* black sheep that cannot produce the billowy clusters of fragrant, sometimes double flowers that mean lilac time in May. Those black sheep, whatever their hue, are listed in the next chapter. This chapter is devoted to the common lilacs and their hybrids, the Chinese and hyacinth lilacs that closely resemble their overwhelmingly popular and populous parent.

Lovers of the common lilac might be sated by the following lists. As E.H. Wilson says in the quotation above, there are "many named sorts" of common lilac. In fact, there are hundreds. The list below includes 15 single whites alone. Gertrude Jekyll had her favorite— see the sidebar on page 74—but how will you choose what to plant in your garden? Start with color, but then consider other features such as fragrance and bloom time and perhaps the ability to bloom where winters are warm. Do you want fall color? Variegated foliage? Do you have a sentimental attachment to the heirlooms developed by the Lemoine family? Or do you want to be patriotic and buy something developed in your own country, maybe in your own province or state? The name alone might beckon like a horse's at the racetrack.

Try to see as many lilacs in bloom as you can. The list below includes most of the cultivars you're likely to find in a catalog or at a garden nursery. Long as it is, the list is far from complete, not only because there are so many kinds but also because more appear every year. Some nurseries produce their own varieties, available nowhere else. For information about a cultivar not listed here, contact the International Lilac Society (see Sources).

*Lilacs marked with an asterisk are recommended for New England gardens by the Arnold Arboretum. In order to make the list, the lilac has to be fragrant, floriferous and resistant to mildew and leaf-roll necrosis.

Released by the Lemoine family in 1891, 'Belle de Nancy' has maintained its popularity for more than a century.

Much as its namesake excelled in lilac breeding, 'Mme Lemoine' dominates a hilltop at the Royal Botanical Gardens.

Syringa x *chinensis*

(formerly *S. rothomagenesis*)

Chinese lilac, Rouen lilac, Rowan lilac

Not Chinese at all, this heavily perfumed hybrid of the cutleaf lilac (*S. protolaciniata*) and common lilac was discovered around 1777 in the botanic garden in Rouen, France. It is a tough, adaptable hybrid, one of five shrubs recommended by the University of Minnesota as capable of surviving there with little or no attention and is thus as suitable for a windbreak or hedge as for a garden's front and center. The Chinese lilac forms a roundish shrub about 12 feet (3.7 m) tall and equally wide. Compared to the common lilac, its dark green leaves are smaller, denser and more disease-resistant, and the small single flowers—lavender on the species—are more delicate and abundant, giving it a lacy appearance in bloom. It suckers less and is later-blooming and thus less susceptible to frost damage to the flower buds. It flowers from zone 3 to 9.

'Bicolor' (Lemoine 1928), known as the Bicolor Chinese lilac, has pale lilac petals with a deep purple eye. (There is also an heirloom common lilac with the cultivar name 'Bicolor.')

'Lilac Sunday'* (Alexander 1997) bears light purple flowers on willowy arching branches.

'Metensis' (origin unknown, ca 1860), also called Rouen lilac, Varin's lilac and 'Pale Chinese,' has very fragrant pale lavender flowers, although shoots may appear bearing creamy white flowers. It is highly susceptible to powdery mildew.

'Red Rothomagensis' (Baldwin pre-1934), which has purple flowers, is used in phenology experiments (see pages 24-25) because it is easily propagated and reproduces true to type.

'Purple Glory' is a hyacinth hybrid developed in California and is thus suited to warmer winters than most lilacs.

'Saugeana' (Saugé ca 1820), the usual form of *S. x chinensis* on the market, also goes by the names 'Rubra,' 'Purple Chinese' and Saugé Chinese lilac. It is a loose, open shrub to 15 feet (4.5 m) tall with very fragrant pinkish to deep reddish purple flowers.

Syringa x hyacinthiflora
Hyacinth lilac, American lilac,
Canadian lilac, Early hybrid
These hybrids resemble *S. vulgaris*, with similar fragrant, single or double flowers, but they sucker less than *S. vulgaris*, flower more reliably on a yearly basis, and their foliage is more attractive in fall, when it turns bronze or burgundy. They bloom earlier than common lilacs, extending the season—thus one common name, the Early hybrids. This means they are vul-

nerable to bud damage by late spring frosts. 'Fénelon' (Lemoine 1937) is the earliest-blooming of all, usually around the first week of May in the northeast.

The *hyacinthiflora* lilacs were created when Victor Lemoine crossed a double form of the common lilac, 'Azurea Plena,' with *S. oblata* subsp. *oblata* in 1876 and named the resulting hybrids for their hyacinth-like double flowers. (Doubles are flowers with more than the usual number of petals.) Only later would Lemoine develop singles, sometimes dubbed Lamartine lilacs in honor of his first one. When Frank Skinner of Dropmore, Manitoba, made the same cross using a different *S. oblata* subspecies, *dilatata*, he produced extremely cold-hardy hybrids—to climatic zone 2. They survive at Beaverlodge, Alberta, where temperatures sometimes drop to -50 or -60 degrees F (-45 to -50°C). Skinner called his hybrids American lilacs, but American nurseries refer to them as Canadian lilacs. These hybrids are generally more compact—to about 10 feet (3 m) tall and almost as wide—and considered overall better-quality lilacs than those of *S. oblata* subsp. *oblata* ancestry, but the advantage of the latter is their ability to bloom in warm-winter areas (zone 9 as opposed to zone 7).

Three Californians, John Sobeck (1894-1965), of Descanso Gardens near Los Angeles, W.B. Clarke (1876-1973), at his nursery in San Jose, and Walter Lammerts (1904-1996), a geologist and plant breeder, took Lemoine's hybrid *S. oblata* subsp. *oblata* further, creating series of hyacinth lilacs which would bloom in that state. Most prized in climatic zones 7 to 9, these 20th-century hybrids retain the fragrance of the common lilac—and its susceptibility to powdery mildew—but gain the ability of *S. oblata* subsp. *oblata* to bloom where winters are short or warm. To encourage these lilacs to bloom, the usual practice is to withhold water from fall until shortly before blooming time, which induces dormancy in the plants. If you live in a cold-winter area (zone 6 or lower), you can grow these lilacs too, but there are probably better choices for your garden. If you do choose a warm-weather lilac, you need not stop watering in the fall.

If the *hyacinthiflora* lilacs seem a bit confusing, gardeners can play it safe by buying cultivars carried by nurseries that cater to their climate.

Cold-Winter *Hyacinthiflora* Lilacs (Zones 2-7)
Hybrids of *S. oblata* subsp. *dilatata* x *S. vulgaris.*

'Asessippi'* (Skinner 1932), often spelled 'Assessippi,' is one of the first lilacs to flower in spring, producing abundant crops of very fragrant pale lilac-colored single flowers on well-shaped upright shrubs as tall as 12 feet (3.7 m).

'Blanche Sweet'* (Fiala 1988), bred from 'Rochester,' is a midseason *hyacinthiflora* that grows to a moderate 7 feet (2.2 m) or so. Bluish buds open into single flowers with a pinkish tint. "An exquisite lilac," according to Select Plus Nurseries.

'The Bride' (Skinner 1961) has single white flowers in panicles as long as 12 inches (30 cm). John Fiala said it was "among the best early-flowering hybrids of this color."

'Churchill'* (Skinner 1945) is an early bearer of single pink flowers.

'Doctor Chadwick' (Skinner pre-1966) has pink buds that open into fragrant single flowers Skinner described as "clear pale sky-blue." This semidwarf grows to only about 8 feet (2.5 m) tall. Twombly Nursery calls it "exceptionally beautiful."

'Evangeline' (Skinner 1934), also called 'Earliest Evangeline,' has dark pink buds that open into double magenta florets that appear contorted.

'Excell'* (Skinner 1935), often spelled 'Excel,' produces great masses of very fragrant single pink flowers.

'Laurentian'* (Skinner 1945) bears single lavender-blue flowers.

'Maiden's Blush' (Skinner 1966) is one of Frank Skinner's most popular lilacs. Its name is shared with a fragrant rose, a good garden companion for this richly fragrant blush-pink lilac that grows about 12 feet (3.7 m) tall. Because it blooms early, it is a good season extender for later-blooming pink *S. vulgaris* cultivars such as 'Lucie Baltet.'

'Mary Short' (Fiala 1979) is a hybrid of 'Pocahontas' x 'Esther Staley' and has profuse crops of double pink florets.

'Minnehaha' (Skinner 1932) has single pinkish flowers.

'Mount Baker' (Skinner 1961), named for the ex-

Hyacinth lilacs such as 'Pink Cloud,' ABOVE, *closely resemble French hybrids such as 'Decaisne,'* FACING PAGE, *but the former sucker less and have better fall color.*

tinct volcano that dominates the horizon in much of the state of Washington, is 8 to 10 feet (2.5-3 m) tall and has such a profusion of single white blooms that the foliage is scarcely visible. In Germany, it is marketed as Schneeweischen™.

'Nokomis'* (Skinner 1934) is an early producer of single lilac-colored flowers.

'Pocahontas' (Skinner 1935) shares the limelight with 'Maiden's Blush' as Frank Skinner's most popular lilac. It can reach 10 to 12 feet (3-3.7 m), so it is a good choice for a specimen, bearing profuse crops of single violet-purple flowers. It is resistant to leaf-roll necrosis.

'Royal Purple' (Skinner 1966) has double flowers that are deep purple with blue centers, for a two-toned

appearance. It forms a densely branching shrub about 6 feet (1.8 m) tall.

'Scotia'* (Scott pre-1942) released by Edith Wilder Scott of Pennsylvania, bears single pink flowers.

'Sister Justina'* (Skinner 1956) bears early crops of highly fragrant brilliant white single flowers.

'Swarthmore' (Skinner 1954) has pinkish buds that open into double mauve flowers streaked with white. Skinner wrote that on the Canadian prairies, this variety "has never failed to flower freely every spring since its introduction."

Warm-Winter *Hyacinthiflora* Lilacs (Zones 3-8)
Hybrids of *S. oblata* subsp. *oblata* x *S. vulgaris*.

'Angel White' (Lammerts 1971), also called 'White Angel,' is a single white that grows rapidly to 12 feet (3.7 m) tall and 10 feet (3 m) wide.

'Big Blue' (Lammerts 1953) is a bluish single.

'Blue Boy' (Sobeck) produces 18-to-20-inch (45-50 cm) panicles of single bluish lavender flowers.

'Blue Hyacinth' (Clarke ca 1942) bears large, loose trusses of single mauve-to-pale-blue flowers.

'Buffon' (Lemoine 1921) has single recurved pinkish lavender flowers and forms a tall shrub. It is highly susceptible to powdery mildew.

'California Rose' (Sobeck) bears great masses of sweetly scented clear light pink single flowers about a week earlier than most pink lilacs.

'Catinat' (Lemoine 1922) has highly fragrant single pink flowers. It is resistant to leaf-roll necrosis.

'Chiffon' (Sobeck) has single lavender flowers.

'Clarke's Giant' (Clarke 1948) is a tall shrub whose rosy mauve buds open into panicles as long as 12 inches (30 cm) of reflexed single lavender-blue florets "so wide it is as if they are trying to show themselves off to the sun," writes Frank Moro of Select Plus Nursery. "Definitely a must for the garden."

'Corinna's Mist' (Moro 2001) is a sport of 'California Rose' with variegated foliage. "This rose has it all," says Frank Moro, who made the selection. "It is suited to warm climates, has exquisite satiny pink fragrant florets and speckled white leaves. It looks like there has been a dusting of snowflakes on it."

'Dark Knight' (Sobeck), also called 'Dark Night' or

Elfe™, bears single velvety purple florets. "It should be used as a focal point in any garden alongside a white or pink lilac," writes Frank Moro of Select Plus Nursery.

'Descanso Princess' (Sobeck) is one of several Sobeck releases whose cultivar names begin with the location 'Descanso,' a public garden near Los Angeles where Sobeck worked as a horticulturist. This lilac has round raspberry-colored buds that open into flowers that are white on the inside and striped burgundy on the outside.

'Esther Staley' (Clarke 1948) is probably the most popular of Clarke's releases. Granted an Award of Garden Merit from the Royal Horticultural Society, it forms a tall shrub with profuse crops of red buds which open into single bright pink flowers. The name commemorates an outstanding California gardener.

'Forrest Kresser Smith' (Sobeck) bears single light lavender flowers. Its cultivar name not only goes under several spellings but may also change gender, becoming 'Mrs. Forrest K. Smith.'

'Lamartine' (Lemoine 1911), which was the first single *hyacinthiflora*, has large panicles of pinkish lilac flowers. The new growth is tinged bronze.

'Lavender Lady' (Lammerts 1953) is the best known of the warm-winter hybrids, with large single rich lilac flowers and intense fragrance. It was used as a parent for Sobeck's Descanso series.

'Louvois'* (Lemoine 1921) bears large single violet flowers.

'Sierra Snow' (Lammerts 1963) bears heavy crops of single flowers with pure white recurved petals. "Of exceptional beauty," writes Select Plus Nurseries.

'Sylvan Beauty' (Sobeck) has single rose-lavender flowers.

'Vauban'* (Lemoine 1913) has highly fragrant double pink flowers. The shrub can grow very large.

'White Angel.' See 'Angel White,' above.

Syringa vulgaris
Common lilac, French hybrid

The lilac against which all other species are measured, *S. vulgaris*, a native of southeastern Europe, is famous, widespread, persistent and naturalized in many parts

'Dappled Dawn' is an American cultivar whose single bluish flowers contrast beautifully with its yellow-variegated foliage.

of the world. Most cultivars are hardy to USDA climatic zone 3, some to warmer parts of zone 2, with the exception of the pink forms, which do best in zones 4 to 7. Lovers of cool winters, some of the common lilacs will nevertheless flower in gardens as warm as zone 8.

In its wild state, a shrub will grow about 12 feet (3.7 m) tall and 8 feet (2.5 m) wide, flowers are fragrant and single, and the usual color is lilac, although there are also white (var. *alba*) and rosy (var. *rubra*) forms. The wide range of colors available today, the double flowers, much larger flower clusters and more compact shrubs are testament to the work of generations of plant breeders.

Although it is easy to grow and maintain, the common lilac has several shortcomings. It isn't a particularly interesting plant after bloom time, with the ex-

ception of the few types with variegated foliage. It doesn't turn color in fall, and the species and most cultivars sucker excessively.

There are several hundred cultivars, all of which— French or not—are sometimes called French hybrids in honor of the pioneering and prolific work done by Victor Lemoine, his wife Marie, their son Emile and grandson Henri from the mid-1800s until the nursery closed in 1955. The following list includes those generally considered most desirable or easiest to find on the market:

'Adelaide Dunbar'* (Dunbar 1916), developed in Rochester, is a historically important American variety with dark stems and double deep reddish purple semi-double florets.

'Agincourt Beauty' (Slater 1973) is an Ontario release with some of the largest florets of the species.

Each violet-purple flower can be as wide as 1.5 inches (4 cm). This showy lilac requires regular pruning to control its upright growth habit.

'Albert F. Holden' (Fiala 1981), named for the founder of the Arnold Arboretum, has unusual coloration, violet-blue on the upper side of the petals and silvery underneath, making the conical florets appear bicolored. The foliage is dark green and the shrub compact, about 7 feet (2.2 m) tall.

'Alice Christianson' (Klager) has double reddish purple flowers. Greer Gardens calls it "a very full-flowering cultivar that reaches a height of 10 to 15 feet (3-4.5 m). Excellent!"

'Alphonse Lavallée'* (Lemoine 1885) bears double lilac flowers with bluish tones.

'Alvan R. Grant' (Fenicchia 1995) is red-purple in bud and opens to fragrant single purple flowers.

'Anabel' (Hawkins 1956), often spelled 'Annabel' or 'Annabelle,' is a very fragrant double pink that blooms at a young age. Roy Hawkins (1886-1972) was an Iowa farmer.

'Andenken an Ludwig Späth' (Späth 1883) goes by several names, most commonly the English translation 'Souvenir of Ludwig Spaeth' or simply 'Ludwig Spaeth'—or Spath. It has long, slender, erect panicles of lightly fragrant single purple flowers that do not fade in the sun. It is widely available and enduringly popular.

'Arch McKean' (Fiala 1984), named for a Michigan lilac specialist, has large, showy dark magenta-purple single flowers shading to violet in the center. Nurseryman Colin Chapman of England says, "What is truly distinctive about this cultivar is the health and vigor which gives it a majestic form and beautiful dark tone. It has a fine green leaf, a strong upright habit and is one of the few lilacs which look better from a distance than close-up."

'Atheline Wilbur' (Fiala 1980) has magenta buds that open into triple multipetaled flowers, violet-blue inside and magenta underneath. Because the florets do not open all at once, each cluster shows a combination of colors. The fragrance has been described as light.

'Aucubaefolia' (Gouchault 1919) is a 'Président Grévy' sport prized for its variegated green-and-yellow foliage.

'Aurea' (unknown origin, pre-1880) is distinguished by foliage that is yellow when young, then turns green in summer. It bears single violet flowers.

'Avalanche' (Fiala 1983) has very large, very fragrant single white flowers on a rounded, compact shrub that eventually grows 9 feet (2.7 m) tall.

Beauty of Moscow. See 'Krasavitsa Moskvy,' below.

'Belle de Nancy' (Lemoine 1891) is one of the most widely available Lemoine cultivars, still considered one of the best double pinks. Purple-red buds open into mauve-pink florets with white centers.

'Beth' (Peterson 1999) was grown from irradiated seed by Nebraska farmer Max Peterson. The slow-growing shrub is dense and bushy, reaching 4 feet (1.2 m) after eight years. It suckers freely. The double flowers are white.

'Biała Anna' (Karpow-Lipski 1971), a European cultivar also called 'Biały Hiacyntowy,' has unusual star-shaped white florets.

Blue Skies®. See 'Monore,' below.

'Bright Centennial' (Robinson 1967) is a Manitoba release that celebrates Canada's centennial. The single flowers are bright magenta.

Burgundy Queen®, whose cultivar name is 'LECburg' (Daniels 1993), has magenta-purple florets similar to those of its parent 'Monge.' It blooms two weeks earlier than most S. vulgaris cultivars, so it can be grown next to 'Monge' for an extension of a similar flowering.

'Catawba Pink' (Utley 1980) has double true pink florets with no lavender. "A real gem," according to Twombly Nursery.

'Catskill' (Lape 1982) forms a smallish shrub 6 feet (1.8 m) tall and not quite as wide. The buds are reddish purple, opening into pale purple flowers.

'Charles Joly'* (Lemoine 1896) is a very fragrant and enduringly popular heirloom, still sometimes considered the best double purple. It earned the Royal Horticultural Society Award of Garden

'Agincourt Beauty,' developed in Ontario, is renowned for the size of its florets, some as wide as 1.5 inches (4 cm).

Merit in 1984. The shrub grows stiffly upright.

'Charles Lindbergh' (Fenicchia 1988), named for the American aviator, has single violet-blue flowers.

'Charm'* (Havemeyer pre-1941) has large single pinkish lilac florets. It blooms young and forms a rounded shrub 8 to 10 feet (2.5-3 m) tall and wide. "Outstanding," says Bailey Nurseries.

'Congo' (Lemoine 1896), sometimes spelled 'Kongo,' is an heirloom that grows about 15 feet (4.5 m) tall. The bright burgundy buds open to single lightly fragrant lilac-purple florets that fade to pale magenta.

'Dappled Dawn' (Hauck 1966) is best known for its variegated foliage, although the single bluish flowers contrast well with the yellow-green leaves. This sport was selected by Cincinnati industrialist Cornelius Hauck.

'Dwight D. Eisenhower' (Fenicchia 1969) is a single multipetaled blue "ranking among the finest blues thus far produced," writes John Fiala. It is somewhat resistant to leaf-roll necrosis.

'Edith Cavell' (Lemoine 1916) bears big clusters of sweetly scented double cream-colored flowers. It can be partnered in the garden with the earlier, whiter 'Miss Ellen Willmott' for extended white bloom. It is highly susceptible to leaf-roll necrosis when grown in areas of high air pollution.

'Edward J. Gardner' (Gardner pre-1950), widely considered one of the best pinks—thus its European moniker, Flamingo™—produces lush panicles of double pale pink star-shaped florets. Select Plus Nurseries writes, "The flower progresses through a subtle range of shades of clear pink as it slowly fades." It blooms better in alternate years.

'Fiala Remembrance' (Margaretten 1991), also known as 'Father John Fiala' and 'John L. Fiala' in honor of the renowned American lilac breeder and author (1924-1990), has cream-colored buds that open into large-petaled double white flowers.

'Flower City' (Fenicchia 1983) is a Rochester lilac that bears single multipetaled violet-purple flowers with a silvery underside. "One of the lilacs of the future," wrote John Fiala in his 1988 book *Lilacs: The Genus Syringa.*

The 19th-century Lemoine hybrid 'Congo,' FACING PAGE, *rates high among magentas, while Wisconsin's 'Edward J. Gardner,'* ABOVE, *is esteemed among the pinks.*

'Frederick Douglass' (Fenicchia 1996) has purple-violet buds that open into single multipetaled blue-violet flowers.

'Frederick Law Olmsted' (Fenicchia 1988) is a vigorous shrub that bears a very heavy crop of small single white flowers. Kent Millham of Highland Botanical Park writes, "From a distance, you can distinguish this cultivar due to the dense array of compact white flowers completely covering the upper portion of the shrub."

'General Sherman'* (Dunbar 1917) bears very fragrant single pinkish flowers that fade to white. "Undoubtedly Dunbar's finest," writes John Fiala.

'Glory'* (Havemeyer 1943) is not a profuse bloomer, but its clusters of large single magenta florets

can be as big as footballs. The profusely suckering shrub can reach 15 feet (4.5 m) tall. "This grand American confidently boasts that size matters," writes Select Plus Nurseries.

'Hallelujah' (Havemeyer and Eaton 1954) is a single magenta selected and named by Mark Eaton from the breeding work of Thomas Havemeyer (1868-1936), an American industrialist whose huge collection of Lemoine lilacs grew on Long Island, New York.

'Henri Robert'* (Lemoine 1936) bears double violet flowers.

'Hippolyte Maringer'* (Lemoine 1909) bears graceful fluffy-looking trusses of double lilac-colored flowers.

'Hugo Koster' (Koster or van Tol 1914) is a Dutch variety with single light reddish purple flowers. It becomes heavily branched at a younger age than many others.

'Hyazinthenflieder'* (Späth 1906), sometimes called the hyacinthflower in direct translation of its German name, bears single lilac flowers.

'Jan van Tol'* (van Tol ca 1916) is a Dutch cultivar that bears giant trusses of single white flowers.

'Jeanne d'Arc'* (Lemoine 1902) bears double white flowers.

'Joan Dunbar'* (Dunbar 1923) bears double white flowers.

'Katherine Havemeyer' (Lemoine 1922) is enduringly popular. Its enormous panicles of highly fragrant double lilac-pink to purplish florets are packed tightly in the clusters. *Hilliers Manual of Trees and Shrubs* (New York, 1972) calls it "quite first class." It is highly susceptible to leaf-roll necrosis when grown in areas of high air pollution.

'Krasavitsa Moskvy'* (Kolesnikov 1947), translated as Beauty of Moscow, is one of many outstanding lilacs from this Russian breeder. Pink buds open into fragrant, lush, densely petaled flowers that are creamy white with shadows of pink. Twombly Nursery says, "One of the finest lilacs in commerce. If you have only one white variety, this should be it." (Don't confuse this with the less highly recommended purple 'Krasnaya Moskva.')

'Léon Gambetta' (Lemoine 1907) has lilac-pink buds that open into graceful clusters of large

'Glory's' few clusters may be as large as footballs.

double lilac-colored flowers, darker outside than inside. This large, upright, mildew-resistant plant is "a must for the lilac collector," say the owners of Twombly Nursery.

'Letha E. House' (Fiala 1990) reaches a compact 6-to-8-foot (1.8-2.5 m) height. It bears dense crops of single pink flowers and blooms in climatic zone 8.

'Little Boy Blue.' See 'Wonderblue,' below.

'Lucie Baltet'* (Baltet pre-1888), pronounced "baltay," one of the favorites of famed English gardener Gertrude Jekyll a century ago, has remained justifiably popular to this day. On a low shrub, coppery buds open into pale pink single flowers.

'Ludwig Spaeth' See 'Andenken an Ludwig Späth,' above.

'Macrostachya' (Renaud 1874), from France, bears large very pale pinkish single flowers on a broadly

More than a century old and still considered one of best pale pinks by fanciers is 'Lucie Baltet.'

spreading shrub. It is also called 'Longcluster.'

'Mme Antoine Buchner'* (Lemoine 1909), whose petals are white suffused with pinkish violet, is often judged the best of the double pinks, with flowers as wide as 0.7 inch (1.7 cm) in dense panicles as long as 10 inches (25 cm). It won the Royal Horticultural Society Award of Merit in 1982.

'Mme Charles Souchet'* (Lemoine 1949) bears large showy clusters of single pale bluish flowers.

'Mme F. Morel'* (F. Morel 1892) bears huge clusters of single dark magenta flowers that maintain their attractiveness as they fade through pale magenta to lilac. Until recently, its clusters were considered the biggest of any lilac.

'Mme Lemoine'* (Lemoine 1890), which honors the wife of famed lilac breeder Victor Lemoine, is a compact heirloom with double white flowers

and dark green foliage. The Royal Horticultural Society *Journal* of 1968 called it "outstanding." It is one of the traditional favorites for forcing.

'Margaret Fenicchia' (Fenicchia 1997) has red-purple buds that open into fragrant purple-violet multipetaled single flowers.

'Marie Frances' (Fiala 1983), which grows just 5 feet (1.5 m) tall, has very fragrant single true pink flowers.

'Marie Legraye'* (Legraye 1879) bears single white flowers. Along with 'Mme Lemoine,' it is one of the traditional cultivars for forcing.

'Martha Stewart' (Fenicchia 1995) bears single bluish violet flowers.

'Maud Notcutt'* (Maarse 1956) grows about 15 feet (4.5 m) tall. It bears large—9-inch (22 cm)— panicles of creamy buds that open into fragrant single pure white flowers, each about an inch (2.5 cm) wide.

'Maurice Barrès'* (Lemoine 1917) produces single bluish flowers.

'Mechta'* (Kolesnikov 1941), spelled various ways and sometimes called the "Dream" lilac, has reddish buds that open into very large panicles of single lilac-blue flowers. "Very showy and dependable," says Weston Nurseries.

'Merlann' (Keaffaber 1975) is a nonsuckering single rose-purple variety that does not fade to bluish.

'Michel Buchner'* (Lemoine 1885) has large, dense panicles of double flowers that open in various shades of lilac. It is still considered one of the best of its color.

'Miss Ellen Willmott'* (Lemoine 1903) has never lost its popularity. Named for a famous English gardener, it has large double pure white florets twice the size of most whites. It is extremely fragrant, blooms dependably and does not sucker excessively.

'Mohawk' (Lape 1982) grows to a moderate 5 feet (1.5 m) tall and not quite as wide. It does not sucker. The buds are dark reddish purple opening to light violet.

'Monge' (Lemoine 1913) has short, broad clusters of large single florets of a rich dark reddish purple.

'Monique Lemoine' (Lemoine 1939), a double white, is "much showier than 'Mme Lemoine' and very fragrant," says Select Plus Nurseries.

'Monore' (Moore 1987), trademarked Blue Skies®, begins to bloom profusely when young, bearing single bluish purple flowers.

'Mrs. Edward Harding' (Lemoine 1922) also goes by

During World War I, 'Paul Thirion,' ABOVE, *was released by Lemoine in France, and 'President Lincoln,'* FACING PAGE, *made history in Rochester, New York.*

the names 'Madame Edward Harding' and 'Mrs. Ed Harding' and may change gender to 'Edward Harding.' This double magenta commemorates Alice Harding,

IN PRAISE OF MARIE

"The lilacs I have are some of the beautiful kinds raised in France, for which we can never be thankful enough to our good neighbors across the Channel. The white variety 'Marie Legraye' always remains my favorite. Some are larger and whiter and have the trusses more evenly and closely filled, but this beautiful Marie fills one with a satisfying conviction as of something that is just right, that has arrived at the point of just the best and most lovable kind of beauty and has been wisely content to stay there, not attempting to pass beyond and excel itself. Its beauty is modest and reserved, and temperate and full of refinement. The color has a deliciously tender warmth of white, and as the truss is not over-full, there is room for a delicate play of warm half-light within its recesses."

—Gertrude Jekyll, *Wood and Garden* (1899)

the author of *Lilacs in My Garden* (Macmillan, 1933).

'Mrs. Harry Bickle' (Rolph 1956), produced by Ontario farmer Harry Rolph, is a single pink with unusually large flowers.

'Mrs. W. E. Marshall' (Havemeyer 1924) is a slow-growing shrub with single very dark purple flowers "the color of eggplant," according to an Italian customer of Ted "Doc Lilac" Marshall. It is highly susceptible to powdery mildew.

'My Favorite' (Klager 1928) was suitably named by its creator, Hulda Klager. It has dark magenta flowers so densely double that they resemble bunches of small grapes when in bud.

'Nadezhda' (Kolesnikov pre-1970) is Russian for "hope." Very large clusters of double florets are lilac-mauve on the outside and pale lilac-blue inside. "One of the best of all the blues," says Twombly Nursery.

'Paul Hariot'* (Lemoine 1902) bears double purple flowers.

'Paul Thirion'* (Lemoine 1915) has squat clusters of deep purple-red buds that open to heavily scented slightly paler magenta flowers. "Truly outstanding," says Twombly Nursery.

'Pink Elizabeth' (Klager), named for plant breeder Hulda Klager's daughter, is described thus by Greer Gardens: "Single flowers in the truss can and do create as much show as their frillier doubled counterparts. The beautiful pink singles of 'Pink Elizabeth' are a testament to this."

'Pixie' (Fiala 1981) is dwarf to semidwarf with single very white flowers.

'Prairie Petite' (Viehmeyer 1998) was grown from irradiated seed at the University of Nebraska. It begins flowering when very young and reaches only about 3 to 4 feet (0.9-1.2 m) tall; single light purple flowers are held in upright clusters.

'Président Grévy' (Lemoine 1886) has large, billowy tresses of double bluish florets, paler on the inside.

'President Lincoln'* (Dunbar 1916) is the most popular of the "blue" lilacs but remains something of a sentimental favorite, as better single blues—that is, with less violet—such as John Fiala's 'Wedgwood Blue'

and 'Wonderblue' have since arrived. Also, its flowers tend to be hidden under its foliage. Nevertheless, it is a lovely lilac.

'Président Loubet' (Lemoine 1901) has fragrant double magenta flowers.

'Président Poincaré' (Lemoine 1913) bears large trusses of reddish buds that open into tightly packed double florets colored lilac and blue. It has "an elegantly refined rather than ostentatious appearance," according to Greer Gardens.

'President Roosevelt'* (Dunbar 1919) bears highly fragrant single purple flowers.

'Primrose'* (G. Maarse 1949), a sport or mutation of 'Marie Legraye' caused by forcing, is the only lilac with any yellow. The small, dense panicles are yellow in bud, opening to single cream-colored florets with shades of yellow fading to white. The subtle coloration of 'Primrose' is more obvious if it is grown next to a white or bluish lilac.

'Reva Balreich' (Peterson 1988) is a dense shrub that reaches 7 feet (2.2 m) and suckers freely. The double flowers are magenta flushed with white, fading to off-white. The progression of opening and fading florets produces a bicolor effect.

'Rochester' (Grant 1971), "perhaps one of the finest single white cultivars ever produced" in the opinion of John Fiala, is a seedling of 'Edith Cavell.' One of its claims to fame is its extensive use as a parent and in crosses with itself to create many successful varieties including 'Arch McKean' and 'Flower City.'

'Ruhm von Horstenstein'* (Wilke 1928) is a German cultivar that forms a large shrub whose highly fragrant bright magenta single flowers bloom early.

'St. Joan' (Blacklock ca 1957) is an exquisite double white from an Ontario horticulturist, Mary Blacklock (1860-1956). John Fiala judged it to be "among the best."

'St. Margaret'* (Blacklock 1953) bears double white flowers. It is marketed in Germany as Frau Holle™.

'Sarah Sands'* (Havemeyer 1943) is a late bloomer with single deep red-purple florets rimmed with a

Yellowish buds will open into the creamy flowers of 'Primrose,' a chemically induced mutant that is the yellowest lilac.

lighter color. It is used extensively for hybridizing. "One of the very finest," writes John Fiala.

'Sensation'* (Eveleens Maarse 1938) is probably the most photographed of lilacs, the first bicolor. This genetic mutant of the lavender 'Hugo de Vries' occurred when the Maarse greenhouse in Holland was forcing lilacs for Christmas flowers. The resulting flowers have deep purple petals margined with white, giving a striking picotee effect. Prune off branches that do not have the bicolor. "*Mon ami,* you must have it for your garden!" writes John Fiala.

'Serene' (Havemeyer and Eaton 1954) is widely considered the most fragrant *S. vulgaris* cultivar. The single flowers are bluish pink.

'Sesquicentennial' (Fenicchia 1972) bears very heavy crops of fragrant single violet flowers.

'Slater's Elegance' (Slater 1983) bears huge single white flowers on plants as tall as 15 feet (4.5 m). "Very difficult to obtain but among the very finest single whites," writes John Fiala.

'Triste Barbaro' (origin unknown, pre-1938) is "one of the darkest purple varieties represented in Highland Park" in Rochester, New York, according to Kent Millham. It is a single.

'Vesper' (Fleming 1981), developed by Robert Fleming at Vineland agricultural station in Ontario, has large single purplish violet flowers.

'Victor Lemoine' (Lemoine 1906) named by Victor Lemoine's son to honor his father, has double lavender-pink flowers that bloom late. "It remains one of the finest to this date," writes John Fiala. "*Bon jardinier,* surely we must find room in our gardens for so fine a lilac and man!"

'Virginité'* (Lemoine 1888) has double pinkish flowers.

'Volcan' (Lemoine 1899), also spelled 'Vulcan,' is one of the darkest purples from Lemoine yet a little paler than 'Andenken an Ludwig Späth.' It has well-exposed single flowers.

'Wedgwood Blue' (Fiala 1981), often misspelled Wedgewood, has pink buds that open to single flowers the color of some English Wedgwood ceramics. The showy flower clusters are held above the foliage of this semidwarf shrub.

Two noteworthy 20th-century lilacs are John Fiala's 'Wonderblue,' or 'Little Boy Blue,' ABOVE, *which is remarkably blue in a world of lilac-tinted hues, and the unique 'Sensation,'* FACING PAGE, *whose bicolored petals spontaneously appeared in a forcing greenhouse in Holland.*

'Wonderblue' (Fiala 1989), or 'Little Boy Blue,' is a semidwarf plant 4 to 5 feet (1.2-1.5 m) tall with exquisite fragrant sky-blue single flowers borne on paired spikes. The leaves are dark green. It is an excellent choice for a container and, along with 'Wedgwood Blue,' one of the best blues.

'Yankee Doodle' (Fiala 1985) is a semidwarf about 8 feet (2.5 m) tall renowned as Fiala's darkest purple. The flowers are single.

'Zhemchuzhina' (origin unknown) has magenta buds that open to clear pink double flowers.

'Zulu'* (Havemeyer pre-1942) bears showy crops of single purple flowers.

Lilac Adventures

Syringa species short and tall, early and late

"All the 23 species more or less accepted today have marvelous tales to tell
of their native lands and the progress made in their development as garden shrubs."
—Fr. John Fiala, *Lilacs: The Genus Syringa* (1988)

As opposed to the common lilacs and their offspring listed in the previous chapter, the lilacs in this chapter are, by and large, garden plants of the connoisseur. Some don't look much like common lilacs at all. They don't necessarily bloom at "lilac time," and they probably don't smell like the lilacs of your childhood. Some smell spicy, some unpleasant, but a couple, most likely to be sniffed out at botanical gardens, are at least as sweetly perfumed as the best of the common lilacs. The flower clusters may be small, the florets oddly shaped. Some are trees. So different are some of these relative newcomers from Asia that they have even fooled scientists, who until the present era of genetic testing, were unsure which plant family should claim them.

But their time has arrived. A few of these once exotic lilacs are showing up at neighborhood nurseries: 'Palibin,' 'Miss Kim,' 'Miss Canada,' Tinkerbelle™ and

the 'Ivory Silk' tree lilac among them. The Prestons, which extend lilac territory northward and lilac season into June, are a lovely, romantically named bunch with a dedicated following of fans that prefer them to all other lilacs.

There are additional species and many cultivars not listed below, but the following are either the most important in hybridizing or those you are most likely to find offered for sale. The specialist lilac nurseries are the best places to find them (see Sources). Look closely, because they may be listed under older or inaccurate botanical names, so frequently have their names changed as identification techniques have improved. Nevertheless, the cultivar names should remain constant.

All flowers listed in this chapter are single.

Syringa amurensis. See *Syringa reticulata* subsp. *amurensis.*

* Lilacs marked with an asterisk are recommended for New England gardens by the Arnold Arboretum. In order to make the list, the lilac has to be fragrant, floriferous and resistant to mildew and leaf-roll necrosis.

'Miss Canada' is a dwarf interspecific hybrid whose complex heritage includes another hybrid, Syringa x prestoniae.

Some of the species lilacs such as the lovely Syringa emodi, ABOVE, *are rarely seen outside of botanical gardens.*

Syringa emodi
Himalayan lilac
This large lilac, discovered in the Himalayas in 1838, forms a robust shrub 15 feet (4.5 m) tall with fairly large oval leaves. Unlike most lilacs, it prefers rich, moist soil and may drop its leaves in a season of drought. The white flowers, which have a fragrance generally described as unpleasant, bloom on erect panicles about three weeks after most *S. vulgaris* lilacs. John Fiala wrote in his book *Lilacs: The Genus Syringa,* "The best specimen is at Highland Park, Rochester, New York, but do not tell them I told you." Sure enough, when I saw that specimen in late May, its delicate flowers with grass-thin white petals bloomed in such abundance that the shrub was a white haze. The Himalayan lilac is resistant to powdery mildew and leaf-roll necrosis. There are two variegated forms, both of unknown origin and both more than a century old: 'Aurea,' also called 'Aurea Villosa'; and 'Aureovariegata,' also labeled 'Variegata.' Both should be given some shade.

Syringa x henryi
This late-flowering hybrid of *S. josikaea* x *S. villosa* was produced by Louis Henry, horticulturist at the Jardin des Plantes in Paris at the end of the 19th century. It is variable and grows tall quickly, to about 10 feet (3 m), so is best planted as a specimen or at the back of the border. Henry's original cultivar is the pale lilac 'Lutèce.' In the 20th century, the reddish 'Julia' (Wickman 1993) was produced in Finland, and white 'Summer White' (Lape 1987), also called 'White Summer' or 'White Summers,' was introduced by Fred Lape, founder of the George Landis Arboretum in New York.

New Hampshire's 'Agnes Smith' is a member of a very winter-hardy group of hybrids, Syringa x josiflexa.

Syringa x josiflexa

These extremely hardy lilacs, to zone 2, are hybrids of *S. josikaea* x *S. komarowii* subsp. *reflexa* created by Isabella Preston in Ottawa. Similar to the Prestons in appearance and bloom time—and often labeled Prestons—they grow upright and flower about two or three weeks later than most *S. vulgaris* forms. They are smaller than the Prestons, however, at about 8 feet (2.5 m) tall. The elongated leaves are dark green, and the fragrant, generally rose-pink, single flowers bloom in loose plumelike panicles. These lilacs are susceptible to witches'-broom. The newest three cultivars listed below come from a lilac-breeding program at the University of New Hampshire.

'Agnes Smith'* (Rogers 1970) has white flowers. It is marketed in Germany as *S.* x *prestoniae* Miss USA™.

'Anna Amhoff' (Yeager 1961) is also white-flowered.

'Bellicent' (Preston pre-1942), which won a Royal Horticultural Society Award of Merit, was Preston's favorite seedling of 'Guinevere.' It has a vigorous but graceful growth habit and enormous panicles of clear rose-pink flowers.

'Elaine' (Preston pre-1953) has white flowers.

'Guinevere' (Preston pre-1942) was described by Isabella Preston as "an attractive plant with large trusses of bloom which show rather more blue in the color than do the *prestoniae* varieties." Its large, loose clusters of flowers open magenta and fade to pinkish lilac. It can reach 10 feet (3 m) tall.

'James Macfarlane' (Yeager 1959) has brilliant pink flowers.

'Redwine' (Morden, Manitoba, pre-1942) has magenta flowers.

'Royalty' (Preston pre-1942), a seedling of 'Guinevere,' grows into a rounded shape about 4 feet (1.2 m) tall and slightly wider. Its clear purple buds open violet-purple.

Syringa josikaea
Hungarian lilac

Along with the far better-known *S. vulgaris*, this is one of two lilac species native to Europe. *S. josikaea* is very different from *S. vulgaris*, however—somewhat less hardy, about zone 3 to 8, less tolerant of drought and poor soil, less fragrant and in bloom almost a month later. And unlike *S. vulgaris*, it has received little attention from plant breeders and gardeners. The Hungarian lilac grows rapidly into a dense rounded shrub about 15 feet (4.5 m) tall and almost as wide. The single flowers, borne in erect panicles, have a deep blue-violet color unique among late-flowering lilacs, but the flower clusters are small. The dark green leaves are large, handsome and glossy. It does not sucker and is hardy and long-lived. It has been used successfully as a hedge plant in places that are not too cold or too dry, and it is sometimes used as a stock for lilac standards.

'Holger' (Tolppola 1975), sometimes called 'Alba,' is a Finnish cultivar with white flowers.

'Kim.' See Interspecific Hybrids, page 96.

'Stropkey Variegated' (Stropkey 1961), selected by an Ohio nurseryman, has pinkish flowers and variegated foliage.

Syringa julianae. See *Syringa pubescens* subsp. *julianae.*

Syringa komarowii
(formerly *S. sargentiana*)
Komarov's lilac, Komarof lilac
This Chinese species is a vigorous shrub about 10 feet (3 m) tall distinguished by oval, textured leaves as long as 8 inches (20 cm). Cylindrical nodding clusters of light pink to deep rose-pink flowers bloom about a month after those of *S. vulgaris.* It reproduces by seeds but seldom suckers. There are two subspecies, *komarowii* and *reflexa.* The latter, called the nodding lilac, is best known as one of the parents of the *josiflexa* and *prestoniae* hybrids.

Syringa x laciniata
(formerly *S. persica* var. *laciniata*)
Feathered Persian lilac
Best known for its relationship with the Persian lilac—although it is not certain as yet which lilac is parent to which—this species is unusual because of its divided foliage. It is pest-resistant and hardy and reliably produces smallish pale lavender blooms every spring around the same time as *S. vulgaris.* Some plants grown under the name of *S. x laciniata* have recently been identified as the similar *S. protolaciniata.*

Syringa meyeri
(formerly *S. velutina, S. palibiniana*)
Meyer lilac, Meyer's dwarf lilac, dwarf Chinese lilac
This species is a natural dwarf that can be kept at about 5 feet (1.5 m) tall or allowed to reach about 8 feet (2.5 m). It is named for Frank Meyer, an employee of the U.S. Department of Agriculture, who was the first westerner to see it. In 1908, he found it growing in a garden near Beijing; it has never been seen growing wild. Meyer reported that the Chinese forced its branches for late winter flowers. *S. meyeri* begins to

bloom when very small and may bloom twice a year, first in spring around the same time as *S. vulgaris,* then again in fall. It is a dependable annual bloomer, capable of flowering from zone 3 to 7 and much less susceptible to powdery mildew and leaf-roll necrosis than is *S. vulgaris.* In fall, its foliage turns dark maroon. Both the species and the cultivar 'Palibin' are included in the Arnold Arboretum's list of 10 favorite uncommon lilacs.

'Palibin'* (unknown origin, pre-1920), previously misnamed *S. palibiniana,* 'Ingwersen's Dwarf' and *S. microphylla minor,* is often dubbed the dwarf littleleaf lilac or the Korean lilac (a name used also for *S. meyeri* and *S. pubescens* subsp. *patula*). 'Palibin' has many good features: glossy green leaves and very fragrant dark pinkish flowers on a shrub that grows slowly and can be kept at a compact 3-foot (0.9 m) height. It stays dense without much pruning, an advantage in a perennial border or hedge. It resists powdery mildew. It suckers somewhat and may also set seeds. This is one of the favorite lilacs of Charles Holetich, retired curator of the lilac garden at the Royal Botanical Gardens in Ontario. See also *S.* 'Bailbelle,' page 95.

'Snowwhite' (Select Plus 2000) has white florets and is advertised by Select Plus Nursery as the first dwarf white lilac.

Syringa microphylla. See *Syringa pubescens* subsp. *microphylla.*

Syringa x nanceiana
Two Lemoine cultivars of this hybrid of *S. x henryi* x *S. sweginzowii* are named *nanceiana* for the city of Nancy, France, where the Lemoine Nursery was located. Both the pink-flowered 'Floréal' (1925) and the purple-flowered 'Rutilant' (1931), sometimes listed as *S. x henryi,* are tall and combine features of both parents.

Syringa oblata
Early lilac, broadleaf lilac
More closely related to *S. vulgaris* than are some other lilac species and similar to it in fragrance, this lilac, whose species name means "widened," is easily distin-

Because it stays small, is disease-resistant and flowers profusely, 'Palibin' is widely available in retail nurseries.

guished by broad, leathery, heart-shaped leaves as wide as 4 inches (10 cm). They turn burgundy or bronze in autumn. Another defining characteristic, the source of its other common name, is its season of bloom. This is one of the earliest lilacs to bloom in spring, ahead of *S. vulgaris*, so even though it is more frost-resistant than *S. vulgaris*, the buds may be damaged by late spring frosts. The flowers are very fragrant. *S. oblata* is tall, about 12 feet (3.7 m), and one of the best species for warm-winter areas, zones 4 to 8.

There are two subspecies, best known as parents of the hyacinth, or early, lilacs. *S. oblata* subsp. *dilatata*, the Korean early lilac, is somewhat smaller and more dense than subsp. *oblata*. The seedling 'Cheyenne' (Hildreth 1971) forms a symmetrical shrub with pink buds that open to highly fragrant pale blue flowers. (See also 'Betsy Ross' under Interspecific Hybrids, page 96.) *S. oblata* subsp. *oblata* (formerly *S. oblata* var. *giraldii*), the purple early lilac, has a more open form, and its panicles are larger, looser and a darker purple. There is a dwarf form, 'Nana.' This subspecies has been used in California to create some of the warm-winter forms of *S.* x *hyacinthiflora* listed in the previous chapter.

Syringa patula. See *Syringa pubescens* subsp. *patula*.

Syringa x persica
Persian lilac

Once assumed to come from Persia, where it has been a garden favorite for centuries, this somewhat small shrub, about 6 to 8 feet (1.8-2.5 m) tall and slightly wider, is a hybrid so ancient that its lineage is unknown. It is assumed to have the common lilac and *S.* x *laciniata* in its background. "The daintiest of all the lilacs," according to Donald Wyman of the Arnold Arboretum, made its way from the Middle East to western Europe and England as early as 1640. It has upright, arching branches, a relatively compact branching habit, attractive bluish green leaves about 2 inches (5 cm) long and early-blooming tubular pale lilac dark-centered flowers with a distinctive spicy fragrance. The flowers are sterile and grow in loose, flat-topped clusters. The plant is resistant to pests and diseases. Like its relative the neem tree of India, the Persian lilac is a source of chromenes, which

are distasteful to insects and can alter their juvenile hormones, so the insects do not mature normally and are not able to multiply. In 11 years of field trials at the University of Minnesota, this species was judged one of the most trouble-free of shrubs, suitable equally for a windbreak or an ornamental garden and capable of thriving with or without irrigation. It flowers from zone 3 to 7. 'Alba' has white flowers.

Syringa pinnatifolia
Pinnate lilac

"So unlike a lilac as to create an amusing 'legpull' or conundrum for the uninitiated" according to *Hilliers Manual of Trees and Shrubs* (New York, 1972), this Chinese lilac has very distinctive feathery-looking pinnate leaves that resemble marigold foliage. It grows about 7 feet (2.2 m) tall and blooms early, producing its small, nodding panicles of white or pale lavender flowers on side buds. E.H. Wilson, who discovered this species in China, described the fragrance as "fetid." However, because of its lovely foliage, it is one of the favorite lilacs of Charles Holetich, retired curator of the Royal Botanical Gardens lilac collection.

Syringa x prestoniae
Preston lilac, Canadian hybrid

Especially popular for their extreme winter hardiness, to zone 2, and their ability to extend lilac season into late May and early June, the Prestons are named for Isabella Preston, who produced not only memorable lilacs but also crabapples, roses and lilies while she was employed by the Canadian government. In 1920, she crossed the late lilac (*S. villosa*) with the nodding lilac (*S. komarowii* subsp. *reflexa*)—hence the drooping panicles—and produced the first of a race of beautiful tall shrubs or small trees that bloom a week to 10 days later than *S. vulgaris*.

Preston's own 71 named releases were succeeded by the work of other breeders, notably Dr. Frank Skinner of Manitoba, but all are labeled *prestoniae*. All bear clusters of long tubular florets that have a unique spicy scent. The shrubs are erect and large, often 10 to 12 feet (3-3.7 m) tall and equally wide. Some have arching branches. Because of their size, Prestons look best in specimen or background roles such as by a fence, in a corner or by a

With its unusually small leaves, Syringa x laciniata *brings a more fragile beauty to the lilac garden than most species.*

wall. They should not be planted too close together or in small areas, but they can be pruned into a tree shape because they produce few or no suckers. The leaves are long and slender (lanceolate) and slightly hairy, making them resistant to leaf miners, although the plants are susceptible to bacterial blight and witches'-broom. Certain cultivars such as 'Agnes Smith,' 'James Macfarlane' and 'Redwine,' sometimes classified as Prestons, are listed under *S.* x *josiflexa*, page 83.

'Alice Rose Foster.' See Interspecific Hybrids, page 95.

'Coral' (Morden, Manitoba, pre-1942) is pure pink.

'Donald Wyman' (Skinner 1944) has dark purple buds that open into wine-red flowers.

'Elinor' (Preston 1928) was described in the early 1900s by Vita Sackville-West, creator of the garden at Sissinghurst, England, as "a most beautiful shrub with tall erect panicles of a deep rose color, opening to a paler shade." She added that it was the only Preston lilac she grew and that others were reported to be just as beautiful. A variegated version has been selected in Britain.

'Helen' (Skinner 1935) has large masses of pinkish white flowers. It is one of the earliest Prestons to bloom.

'Hiawatha' (Skinner 1932) has reddish purple buds that open pale pink.

'Isabella' (Preston pre-1942), named for its creator, is a pyramidal shrub with large clusters of lilac-pink flowers that are almost white inside.

'Jessica' (Preston pre-1942) is one of the latest and darkest of Preston's releases, with fragrant violet flowers.

'Miss Canada.'* See Interspecific Hybrids, page 96.

'Nike' (Bugala 1970) is a Polish release whose dark violet buds open into violet flowers. It is reputed to be the darkest Preston.

'Nocturne' (Morden, Manitoba, pre-1942) is a

Its buds opening as the French hybrids fade, a Preston lilac such as 'Nike' extends lilac season by a couple of weeks.

smallish Preston about 5 feet (1.5 m) tall and wide. The fragrant flowers are pale blue.

'Silvia' (Preston pre-1928) bears heavy crops of pink flowers.

'Virgilia' (Preston 1928) has a compact habit and deep lilac-magenta buds that open pale lilac.

Syringa protolaciniata
(formerly *S. afghanica*)
Cutleaf lilac, fernleaf lilac
The common names and the Latin *laciniata*, meaning "torn," describe deeply serrated leaves that resemble fern leaves—very different from the foliage of other lilacs. They give a delicate look to this roundish shrub about 8 feet (2.5 m) tall and wide. The cutleaf lilac is attractive in three seasons and suited to almost any garden as a specimen, hedge or border plant

and provides a colorful accent in a Japanese-style garden. Many small clusters of fragrant lilac-colored flowers bloom around the same time as *S. vulgaris*. The seeds are fertile, so it may self-sow. Awarded a Royal Horticultural Society Award of Merit in 1965 and included in the Arnold Arboretum's list of 10 favorite uncommon lilacs, it will grow in the southern states to zone 8 as well as in the north to zone 4.

'Kabul' (origin unknown) grows only about 3 feet (0.9 m) tall and has violet flowers.

Syringa pubescens
Hairy lilac
This dwarf Chinese shrub—3 to 6 feet (0.9-1.8 m) tall—and the three subspecies that follow are named for their leaves, which are about 0.5 to 1.5 inches (1-3.8 cm) long and hairy underneath, thus slightly

Josée™ yields bumper crops of sweetly fragrant flowers.

introduced in 1900, this subspecies, hardy to zone 3, was described as "one of the loveliest lilacs" by John Fiala in *Lilacs: The Genus Syringa*. *Hilliers Manual of Trees and Shrubs* calls it "ideal for the small garden." This graceful, upright-branching shrub 4 to 8 feet (1.2-2.5 m) tall and equally wide has small oval leaves, glossy dark green above and downy grey underneath, that resemble those of privet. It is pest- and mildew-resistant. The sweetly fragrant flowers, which bloom later than those of S. *vulgaris*, are borne in slender, upright panicles. They are deep purple outside and white inside, "so as the flowers open, the inflorescence is purple and white in pleasing contrast," wrote Wilson.

'George Eastman' (Fenicchia pre-1978), named for a founder of the Kodak corporation, has red buds that open into rose-pink florets.

'Hers,' discovered in China by Joseph Hers in 1923, is a rare weeping lilac. It grows about 5 feet (1.5 m) tall and at least twice as wide, the tips of the delicate arching branches trailing on the ground. The branches can be trained to grow on a trellis. Abundant crops of small fragrant lavender single flowers bloom dependably every year.

soft to the touch. All grow slowly, so they are good choices for small gardens and low hedges. Because the pale purplish lilac flowers bloom later than those of S. *vulgaris*, they are seldom lost to spring frosts. Ernest H. Wilson of the Arnold Arboretum, who brought many lilac species from China to North America, judged S. *pubescens* the "most fragrant of all lilacs." It does not sucker, requires little or no pruning and is resistant to mildew and leaf-roll necrosis. Several subspecies are important in gardens. All except the less hardy subspecies *pubescens* (zone 4 to 8) will bloom from zone 3 to 8. See also Josée™, page 96.

Syringa pubescens subsp. *julianae*
(formerly S. *julianae*)
Juliana lilac
Discovered by E.H. Wilson in western China and

Syringa pubescens subsp. *microphylla*
(formerly S. *microphylla*)
Littleleaf lilac, Daphne lilac
Delicate branches bear small mildew-resistant leaves and very fragrant lilac-colored flowers that bloom in May or June and intermittently until fall—thus a Chinese name for it, the Fourseason Lilac. In that country, biologist Joseph Hers (whose name is remembered in the 'Hers' lilac, above) recorded that the flowers were used to make a tea. Like the other members of this species, it is very fragrant. A couple of shrubs at the entrance to the lilac dell at the Royal Botanical Gardens in Ontario welcome visitors like perfumed hostesses at a classy party.

'Superba' (Cassegrain 1933) won the Royal Horticultural Society Award of Merit and is one of the Arnold Arboretum's 10 favorite uncommon lilacs. It bears profuse crops of pale pink flowers.

Syringa pubescens subsp. *patula*

(formerly *S. palibiniana, S. patula, S. velutina*)
Dwarf Korean lilac, Manchurian lilac
The attractive mildew-resistant glossy dark green leaves turn burgundy in fall, and the branches form an attractive shape in winter. This subspecies is also climatically versatile, capable of flowering every spring in any zone from 2 or 3 to 8. In the southern United States, it should be given morning sun and afternoon shade and mulched with shredded bark to keep the soil cool. Water deeply every four to six weeks in dry weather.

'Cinderella' (Select Plus 1998) is similar to the better-known 'Miss Kim,' but the flowers are pink.

'Miss Kim'* (Yeager 1954), also called 'Katinka,' was brought to the United States in 1947 as seed from South Korea by Professor E.M. Meader of the University of New Hampshire, who chose to name his selection in honor of "a most common family name in Korea. There are thousands of Misses Kim, and many could easily win a beauty contest." This 'Miss Kim' has purple buds that open to highly fragrant lavender flowers. Blooming begins later than other lilacs and continues over a long period. It flowers reliably every year and makes a good low hedge.

Syringa pubescens subsp. *pubescens*

(formerly *S. villosa* var. *pubescens*)
This lilac forms a neat shrub only 6 to 8 feet (1.8-2.5 m) tall. It is less hardy than most, to about zone 5; the young growth and flower buds may be injured by late frosts. The flower are pale lilac to violet and extremely fragrant.

Syringa reticulata subsp. *amurensis*

(formerly *S. amurensis, S. reticulata* var. *mandschurica*)
Amur lilac, Manchurian lilac, Siberian lilac
A native of China, where it has been grown in temple gardens for centuries, this tree lilac and the closely related subspecies that follow are only now assuming their rightful place among ornamental trees in North America. At 10 to 16 feet (3-5 m), the Amur lilac is generally shorter and shrubbier than either the Peking or Japanese tree lilac, and its smaller leaves are hairless

underneath. When allowed to grow several stems, it has been used successfully as a hedge. Its chief landscape value is its showy 6-inch-long (15 cm) panicles of whitish flowers that open about a month after those of *S. vulgaris* but before the other *S. reticulata* subspecies. It is hardy to zone 2.

'Falconskeepe' (origin unknown), named for John Fiala's garden Falconskeape, is described by ArborVillage as a more prolific bloomer and better plant than the subspecies.

Syringa reticulata subsp. *pekinensis*

(formerly *S. pekinensis, Ligustrum pekinensis*)
Peking lilac
This subspecies, one of the first lilacs brought to Europe from China, having been found near Beijing in 1742 by the French Jesuit priest Pierre d'Incarville, blooms after the subspecies *amurensis* and before the *reticulata*. It has distinctive papery exfoliating bark and dark green fine-textured foliage. It grows quite rapidly into a slender round-topped shrub or small tree that may take years to bloom after planting. Resistant to diseases and pests and needing little or no pruning, it is included in the Arnold Arboretum's list of 10 favorite uncommon lilacs. It is hardy to zone 4.

'Morton' (Bachtell 1994), also known as 'Chicago Tower' and the China Snow™ lilac (formerly Water Tower®), is a Morton Arboretum selection introduced by Chicagoland Grows Inc. in the 1990s. The original tree, which has golden bark, is 40 feet (12 m) tall and 35 feet (10.5 m) wide.

'Pendula' (Temple 1887) is a weeping form.

'Summer Charm' (Wandell 1992), which also has the unpoetic cultivar name 'DTR 124' and the trademark name Summer Charm™, grows 15 to 20 feet (4.5-6 m) tall and not quite as wide.

Syringa reticulata subsp. *reticulata*

(formerly *S. amurensis* var. *japonica, S. japonica*)
Japanese tree lilac, Hara Japanese tree lilac
An esteemed lilac in its native northern Japan, where the wood was traditionally used in the creation of cer-

The Japanese tree lilac is so different from its shrubby kin that it was not positively classified until recently.

emonial wands "regarded as guardians against disease, evil spirits and dangers of all kinds," according to E.H. Wilson, this neat, small tree has attained sudden popularity in North America. Recommended for small gardens and for street or median plantings from about zone 3 to 8, it flowers profusely, resists diseases and air pollution and tolerates poor, alkaline and salty soils. Top marks have come from the Arnold Arboretum, the University of Maine and the Ontario Ministry of Agriculture and Food, which called it "the most pest-free lilac" in its 1984 pamphlet "Small Trees for Small Spaces."

This large shrub (if the lower branches are not pruned off when young) or small tree forms a vase shape and is graceful with or without leaves. It grows slowly to 18 to 35 feet (5.5-10.5 m) and has a broad oval crown about 15 feet (4.5 m) wide. This is the latest-blooming of all lilacs, sometimes flowering into July, producing large, loose panicles of creamy white flowers. The late flowering means that its flower buds are the least likely to be harmed by late frosts. The foliage is coarse and dark green. The bark is speckled, glossy and reddish brown, similar to that of cherry. On the negative side, it is fairly susceptible to breakage from winter ice, and its flowers do not have the characteristic lilac fragrance. In colder parts of Alberta or where winter temperatures are varied, it has suffered from tip kill or has died back to the ground. The variegated forms should be given partial shade to prevent scorching of the leaves.

'Argentea' (Temple pre-1917) has foliage that opens golden.

'Cameo's Jewel' (Select Plus 1989) has foliage that is mottled and margined yellow and marked with cream by midsummer.

'Chantilly Lace' (Herrmann 1987) has irregularly margined pale yellow-green leaves that become creamy yellow as they mature.

'China Gold' (Fiala 1955), selected from chemically treated seeds, is more upright and narrow than the others. It grows to about 25 feet (7.5 m). The new stems are reddish and the new foliage light yellow, turning pale yellow-green or green by summer.

'Golden Eclipse' (Bakker 2002) has variegated foliage—two shades of green in spring that gradually

The buds of Syringa reticulata *subsp.* amurensis *do not bloom until about a month after traditional lilac season.*

change over the summer to green and yellow.

'Ivory Silk' (Pokluda 1973) is something of a phenomenon. This release from Sheridan Nurseries in Ontario has received such favorable publicity that nurseries can hardly keep it in stock. One of four woody ornamentals given a gold medal in 1996 by the Pennsylvania Horticulture Society, it forms a rounded shape about 20 to 25 feet (6-7.5 m) tall and 15 feet (4.5 m) wide, more narrow and compact than the others. The leaves are dark green. The flowers, which are creamy white and begin to appear when the shrub is young, bloom earlier than those of most *reticulata* cultivars, between mid-June and early July.

Regent™, whose cultivar name is 'PNI 7523' (Flemer 1988), may be variable because according to the *International Register of Cultivar Names of the Genus Sy-*

Syringa tomentella is a strong-growing species whose grayish bark develops distinctive knobby lenticels.

ringa (Vrugtman, 2001), the plants are grown from seed.

'Summer Snow' (Schichtel 1980) is a slow-growing selection that is shorter than the others at maturity and forms a rounded head.

Syringa x swegiflexa
Chengtu nodding lilac

This beautiful strong-growing hybrid of S. *komarowii* subsp. *reflexa* x S. *sweginzowii* was created in Germany around 1934. The dark green leaves are large, oval and resistant to powdery mildew. Large, dense, cylindrical drooping panicles of flowers are generally red in bud and pink when open. Capable of flowering from zone 3 to 8, this shrub grows 9 to 12 feet (2.7-3.7 m) tall and somewhat wider.

'Fountain' (Preston pre-1953) is medium-sized and compact and has long, drooping panicles of pale pink flowers that bloom around the same time as those of S. *vulgaris.*

Syringa sweginzowii
Chengtu lilac

This Chinese species grows into an erect shrub 5 to 9 feet (1.5-2.7 m) tall with leaves about 2 to 3 inches (5-7.5 cm) long. The flowers, which have a spicy fragrance, are lilac to reddish and bloom in long, loose panicles later than those of S. *vulgaris.* The *Bulletin* of the Arnold Arboretum of 1912 declared this species "one of the loveliest of all lilacs." In the garden, the species is most likely to be represented by its hybrids, such as S. x *henryi*, S. x *swegiflexa*, S. x 'Lark Song' and S. x *nanceiana*.

Syringa tomentella
(formerly S. *wilsonii*)
Felty lilac

This strong-growing, wide-spreading western Chinese shrub reaches 10 to 15 feet (3-4.5 m) and bears broad panicles of sweetly scented pink- to rose-colored flowers just after S. *vulgaris* blooms. When E.H. Wilson first saw this species blooming in Tibet in 1908, he "thought that I had never seen so handsome a species of lilac." The species name, which means woolly, describes the foliage, which is large, corrugated and dark green above, downy grey underneath. It does not sucker.

'Kum-Bum' (Fiala 1969) is named for a monastery in China where, according to legend, the first tree of S. *reticulata* subsp. *pekinensis* grew. Also called 'Aurea Tomentella,' it is a chemically induced tetraploid with violet flowers and golden foliage that turns green in summer. Plant it in sun for full leaf color.

Syringa villosa
Late lilac

This Chinese species, discovered by the French missionary Pierre d'Incarville in 1750, is best known for its understudy role as one of the parents of S. x *prestoniae*. "The flowers are rose-colored, pink or nearly white, but have an unpleasant odor," wrote plant explorer E.H. Wilson. "It is, however, a first-rate garden shrub, exceedingly floriferous, very valuable for its har-

Unusual species such as Syringa tomentella, FACING PAGE, *and S.* wolfii, ABOVE, *are attracting more attention.*

diness and for its late flowers." Alice Harding, author of *Lilacs in My Garden*, said it was her favorite of the species lilacs. It is hardy to zone 2, drought-tolerant, blooms reliably every year and is tough enough to make a sturdy hedge about 12 feet (3.7 m) tall. Its bloom time is about halfway between those of the common lilac and the last of the tree lilacs. It is fairly tolerant of salty soil and resistant to leaf-roll necrosis and powdery mildew but susceptible to bacterial blight.

'Onarga' (origin unknown, pre-1951) has pink flowers.

Syringa wolfii
(formerly *S. formosissima, S. robusta*)
Wolf lilac
This Mongolian species is extremely winter-hardy, to zone 2. It forms a large, open shrub and flowers when young. The spring growth is tinged reddish brown, the branches ash-gray. The leaves are pointed and 3 to 5 inches (7.5-12 cm) long. Fragrant lavender-blue flowers are borne on long, loose panicles about a month after those of *S. vulgaris*. See also 'Hagny,' page 96.

Syringa yunnanensis
Yunnan lilac
This is a beautiful medium-to-large shrub, sometimes 12 feet (3.7 m) tall, with a loose, open habit. The leaves are grayish underneath. Pink buds open into fragrant lilac-pink flowers that fade as they age. It does not sucker and is resistant to many diseases, including leaf-roll necrosis and powdery mildew.

'Prophesy' (Fiala 1969) is a tetraploid with larger and deeper lavender-pink flowers than those of the species. It has been used as a flowering screen.

INTERSPECIFIC HYBRIDS
These lilacs, mostly modern, are the playthings of plant breeders and geneticists. They are the results of combining at least two species. Some interspecific hybrids have been given their own species name, such as *S. x nanceiana, S. x prestoniae* and *S. x josiflexa*, all listed on previous pages. The following do not belong to any group, and although they're all gathered together here, they do not necessarily resemble one another.

'Alexander's Pink' (Alexander 1967) is a hybrid of *S. x josiflexa* 'James Macfarlane' x *S. x prestoniae* 'Ethel M. Webster.' This lilac from a Massachusetts nursery owner has bright pink flowers.

'Alice Rose Foster' (Alexander 1968), sometimes classified as a Preston—it has the same parentage as 'Alexander's Pink,' above—is one of the favorites of Charles Holetich of the Royal Botanical Gardens lilac collection. It tolerates extreme cold, has unusual elongated leaves and flowers in a combination of rose, pink and white.

'Anastasia' (Select Plus 1996), a hybrid of *S. pubescens* subsp. *microphylla* x *S. meyeri*, is a dwarf shrub with magenta florets.

'Bailbelle' (Bailey Nurseries 2000), better known as the Tinkerbelle™ lilac, was the first of the Fairytale series of lilacs to be released by Bailey Nurseries, a

U.S. wholesaler. This Dutch hybrid of *S. meyeri* 'Palibin' x *S. pubescens* subsp. *microphylla* 'Superba' is a small-leafed dwarf that grows slowly to about 5 to 6 feet (1.5-1.8 m) tall and wide. It starts to flower when only a foot (30 cm) tall, producing wine-red buds that open into pink flowers with a spicy fragrance. It is hardy from zone 3 to 7. While this form can be cut back to 8 inches (20 cm) for rejuvenation, there is also a tree form, grafted onto *S. reticulata*, that reaches an eventual height and width of 5 feet (1.5 m).

'Betsy Ross' (Egolf 1992) grows to about 10 feet (3 m) tall and 13 feet (4 m) wide; it produces dark green foliage and large crops of fragrant pure white flowers. Released by the U.S. National Arboretum to the commercial trade in 2000, it is mildew-tolerant and adapted to both the northern and the southern United States. One parent is *S. oblata*.

'Ferna Alexander' (Alexander pre-1970), with the same heritage as 'Alexander's Pink' and 'Alice Rose Foster,' above, has spicy-smelling satin-pink florets.

'Hagny' (Olsen and Gram 1935) is a Danish hybrid of *S. wolfii* x *S. reflexa*. It forms a large shrub with dense crops of pure pink flowers.

Josée™ (G. Morel 1974) is the trademark name for the cultivar 'MORjos 060F.' Also called 'Jenny,' this French hybrid of *S. pubescens* subsp. *microphylla* x *S. pubescens* subsp. *patula* grows only about 4 to 5 feet (1.2-1.5 m) tall and may bloom as often as four times in a season. The pale pink flowers are sweetly fragrant.

'Kim' (Preston pre-1942), sometimes listed as *S. x prestoniae*, is an elegant medium-sized shrub with dark green leaves and deep lilac flowers. One parent is *S. josikaea*. It should not be confused with *S. pubescens* subsp. *patula* 'Miss Kim,' page 90.

'Lark Song' (Fiala 1968) has *S. sweginzowii*, *S. tomentella* and *S. komarowii* in its heritage. This is a semidwarf that grows 6 to 12 feet (1.8-3.7 m) tall and bears heavy crops of long tubular medium-pink florets.

'Minuet' (Cumming 1972) is a hybrid of *S. x josiflexa* 'Redwine' x *S. x prestoniae* 'Donald Wyman' released by Dr. William Cumming (1911-1999) from the Morden Arboretum in Manitoba. It is a dense, compact, nonsuckering dwarf about 5 to 6 feet (1.5-1.8 m) tall with large dark green leaves. The light lavender

Although quite different, the dwarf lilacs, ABOVE, *are all suitable for container culture: 'Minuet,' left, 'Miss Kim,' center, and 'Palibin,' right.* FACING PAGE: *'Palibin.'*

flowers resemble those of the Preston lilacs.

'Miss Canada' (Cumming 1967) is sometimes called the Pink Lilac in honor of its bright pink flowers that open from deep red buds in late May or early June. This hybrid of *S. x josiflexa* 'Redwine' x *S. x prestoniae* 'Hiawatha' is sometimes classified as a Preston. It forms a spreading shrub 6 to 9 feet (1.8-2.7 m) tall. In his book *Lilacs: The Genus Syringa*, John Fiala called it "a triumph of Canadian hybridizing for an outstanding beauty."

'Sleeping Beauty' (Moro 2001) is a hybrid of *S. pubescens* subsp. *microphylla* 'Superba' x *S. meyeri* 'Palibin' by the owner of Select Plus Nursery in Quebec. This dwarf shrub has pink florets and reddish fall foliage.

'Spellbinder' (Fiala 1968), a hybrid of *S. komarowii* x *S. wolfii*, is a tetraploid with single pink flowers.

Lilac Aid

Or Why won't it bloom?

"READ THE RESPONSE OF THE PLANT. LET THE BOOKS YOU READ,
THE LECTURES YOU ATTEND, THE FRIENDS YOU CONSULT BE A GUIDELINE ONLY.
RETURN TO THE PLANT AND LEARN HOW TO READ ITS STATE OF HAPPINESS, SURVIVAL OR SUFFERING."
—Charles Holetich, Former Curator, Royal Botanical Gardens Lilac Collection

Given their few requirements, lilacs tend toward happiness and survival rather than suffering. As William T. Councilman wrote in Susan Delano McKelvey's *The Lilac: A Monograph*, "There are many reasons for the persistence of the lilac, among them the fact that it has few parasites or other natural enemies....The foliage is apparently not affected by many species of leaf-eating insects, and it generally maintains a good healthy condition throughout the season, except that it is sometimes affected by disfiguring fungi in late summer and autumn."

That sums up lilac health in a nutshell. Nevertheless, a happy, surviving lilac need not be a blooming one.

WHY WON'T IT BLOOM?

There are several possible answers, most of which have nothing to do with diseases or pests.

1. Perhaps your plant is taking a sabbatical. Many lilacs don't bloom at all until they are several years old. Some lilacs, especially cultivars of the common lilac (*S. vulgaris*) bloom better—or only—in alternate years. Pruning the plant soon after it does bloom may encourage flowers next year.

2. The next most common problem is pruning too late—or too early. In summer, the flower and leaf buds form for next year. If you prune in summer or any time before the flowers bloom, you will cut off next spring's show. The best time is right after the blossoms fade.

3. Maybe you fertilized too much or used the wrong fertilizer. Lilacs can grow and bloom on poor soil, so too much fertilizer is more likely to cause harm than too little. Too much nitrogen can cause excessive suckering, lessen winter hardiness, increase vulnerability to pest and disease damage and reduce or stop flowering. The nitrogen fertilizer may not have been applied to the lilac directly but to the lawn or flowerbeds above the roots. Either don't fertilize a lilac at all, or in spring after blooming time, give it a light applica-

The fabulous annual blooming of this 'Monge' lilac is evidence of well-situated planting and conscientious care.

The loss of chlorophyll apparent in the foliage seen here may have been caused by the drift from herbicide spraying.

tion of a fertilizer with a high middle number such as 4-12-8—that is, a fertilizer high in phosphate. Pets urinating on or by the lilac can also cause an overbalance of nitrogen.

4. Perhaps your lilac isn't receiving its requisite six hours of sun a day. Maybe you planted it in sun, but its environment has changed in the meantime because of construction or the growth of surrounding plants. You may need to thin overshadowing trees or relocate the lilac.

5. Root damage can cause the plant to stop flowering until it builds up its strength. The damage may have occurred during planting, construction or nearby digging.

6. Maybe the soil is not well drained. In this case, the entire plant will appear leggy and unhealthy and may die.

7. On the other hand, prolonged drought can cause blossoms to drop and leaves to wilt, brown at the edges and drop prematurely. Drought may have occurred the year before you notice the lack of bloom. Since most lilacs are drought-resistant, you are likely to see symptoms of drought damage first on other plants in your garden. Water mature plants deeply if there is no rain for more than two weeks. Newly planted shrubs need watering once a week in dry weather.

8. Perhaps your climate is too harsh for the type of lilac you've chosen. A lilac that is not sufficiently hardy may suffer from tip dieback or may be killed right to the ground. Even if it survives the winter, its flower buds can be killed by late spring frosts following a period of warm weather. The lilacs most likely to bloom where winters are long include the Prestons,

The highly fragrant Syringa pubescens *'Superba' is among the best choices in places where winters are long and severe.*

S. x *josiflexa*, S. *meyeri*, S. x *chinensis*, S. x *persica*, any of the S. *pubescens* lilacs, S. *villosa*, S. *wolfii* and later-blooming cultivars of S. *vulgaris*.

9. On the other hand, lilacs that require cold winters may not bloom in climatic zone 7 or warmer. Check local nurseries for lilacs known to bloom there, such as 'Miss Kim,' 'Palibin,' 'Betsy Ross,' S. *oblata*, S. *proto-laciniata* and certain varieties of S. x *hyacinthiflora*.

10. If a lilac that once bloomed profusely is now sparse, ageing may be the problem. The plant may need renewing (see pages 37-39).

11. Diseases can lessen or stop blooming. An infection may have occurred the previous year and destroyed the flower buds. In some cases, preventive or curative

measures can be taken, but location is very important. While dry rural gardens may have perfectly healthy lilacs, lilacs in big cities are susceptible to leaf-roll necrosis. Lilacs in places with dry summers and cold winters are more likely to remain disease-free than those growing where conditions are humid and winters are mild. In all cases, selection of a resistant species or cultivar is the best assurance of bloom.

12. Lastly, pest problems, especially scale or borers, can cause a lilac to bloom less. The common lilac (S. *vulgaris*) and its many cultivars are among the most susceptible to pests.

Stresses that can harm plants—though they may not stop blooming entirely—can be grouped into two types: abiotic and biotic. The first 10 points listed above are called abiotic stresses because they are caused by nonliving influences. Biotic stresses are those caused by living things such as insects, animals, bacteria, and such.

ABIOTIC STRESSES

These stresses can be harder to diagnose and treat than biotic stresses because their symptoms are wide-ranging and often similar.

Girdling injury: Barking of the stems with machinery, usually lawn mowers or string trimmers, goes under the umbrella term "Jim injury." If the bark is removed all the way around a stem, it will die. Mice, deer and rabbits may do this in winter, but a wire or even a string tied around a branch or stem can be as harmful, because that part of the plant will strangle as it grows. Remember to remove the label from your lilac and any string around the stem. If you spot girdling injury early, you may be able to save the stem by bridge-grafting across the damage as described in books on grafting.

Herbicide injury: Drift from sprays meant to kill weeds in lawns or flower borders can cause lilac leaves to discolor and drop.

Pollution injury: Disorders that cause leaves to literally curl up and die are grouped under the heading LRN, leaf-roll necrosis. Because this is a largely a problem of city lilacs, it is thought to be caused by air pollution. In May or June, the leaves roll or curl, develop scorch marks, brown underneath and fall early in the season, sometimes to be replaced by new leaves. In a trial at Brooklyn Botanical Garden, all cultivars of *S. vulgaris* were moderately or severely injured; 'Edith Cavell' and 'Katherine Havemeyer' were especially susceptible.

BIOTIC STRESSES

Diseases

Blight: Symptoms of bacterial blight (*Pseudomonas syringae* var. *syringae*) generally show up early in the season, during or directly after a spell of hot, humid weather. The onset can be dramatic. Leaves suddenly look scorched along the edges, then young shoots blacken. Leaves may also have dark spots surrounded by

Leaf-roll necrosis, ABOVE, *is largely a problem in cities, so it is presumed to be caused by air pollution. Some species such as* Syringa yunnanensis, FACING PAGE, *are resistant.*

a pale halo. Flower clusters wilt and die. The same strain also infects pear, cherry, maple and other ornamentals.

Another type of blight, caused by the fungus *Ascochyta syringae*, shows similar symptoms and spreads up from the soil in the wet weather of early spring. These blights will not kill the plant but are unsightly and can destroy much of the new growth. Depending on the timing of the infection, blooms may be lost this season or next.

Control is difficult. Wounded plants and new growth are most susceptible. Provide excellent air drainage to reduce frost damage and dry the foliage. Damage is worse in low-lying areas, where cold, damp air can pool. If you can catch blight early, remove all

Lilacs can briskly proceed from healthy, FACING PAGE, *to scorched in a matter of days if they are infected by bacterial or fungal blight,* ABOVE, *both of which are most common on susceptible species in hot, humid weather.*

infected parts by cutting into the healthy growth below them, always sterilizing the pruning shears or saw between cuts with rubbing alcohol, Lysol or a solution of 1 part household bleach to 10 parts water. Next year, use a copper fungicide spray when spring weather is warm and wet and thus favorable for infection. Avoid heavy pruning and excessive fertilizing, practices that encourage rapid, weak growth. Early-blooming lilacs such as *S.* x *hyacinthiflora* and the earliest *S. vulgaris* cultivars are most susceptible; singles are more susceptible than doubles; and plants with magenta, purple and blue flowers are more susceptible than those with lilac colors. *S. komarowii, S.* x *prestoniae* and *S. villosa* are also susceptible, although most

late-blooming species and cultivars are more resistant.

Mycoplasma: Witches'-broom, a disease more common in large lilac collections than on backyard shrubs, appears as a clump of very dense growth on an otherwise ordinary tree or shrub. First noted in 1951, the disease is still somewhat mysterious, although it is known to be caused by a class of viruslike pathogens called MLO (mycoplasma-like organisms, or mollicutes). Apparently, the organisms colonize in the sap (phloem), interrupting its flow and thus killing a growing point, which results in the dense growth of side shoots, usually low down on the plant. The late-flowering lilacs, particularly *S.* x *josiflexa* and *S.* x *prestoniae*, are most susceptible. The shrub may look unhealthy, have twiggy growth and uncharacteristic out-of-season bloom or growth flushes and eventually die. A similar disease of ash trees called ash yellows can infect healthy lilacs and vice versa, probably via an insect. Pruning with sterilized tools is important. Dip or wipe the blades in rubbing alcohol, Lysol or a solution of 1 part household bleach to 10 parts water before you move to another plant. There is no known cure. Remove and destroy plants with obvious symptoms.

Powdery mildew: The disease that almost eliminated lilacs in areas of the Pacific northwest and the Canadian West Coast is caused by a fungus (*Microsphaera alni, M. syringae*) that hits when the air is warm and humid. It usually starts on older leaves toward the base of the plant in July and spreads throughout the foliage from mid-August until the leaves fall in October. Leaves develop unsightly white or light gray patches, then turn yellow and drop off. New growth may be stunted. The damage is more aesthetic than physiological, as it usually occurs when the leaves have fulfilled their purpose.

The best defenses come at planting time (see Chapter 2). Give lilacs full sun and air circulation and, if possible, choose resistant cultivars and species. Try to avoid wetting the foliage any more than necessary. Irrigate deeply by watering directly on the ground. Most *S. vulgaris* cultivars and hybrids are susceptible; the worst include 'Buffon,' 'Henri Martin,' 'Marlyensis' and 'Mrs. W.E. Marshall.' *S.* x *chinensis* 'Metensis' is also susceptible. If your plants tend to become in-

Pruning of all crowded and infected wood is the best way to prevent and control diseases that stunt foliage and flowers.

fected, grow them behind perennials such as lilies and ornamental grasses that are tallest when the lilacs are disfigured. Resistant species include S. x *diversifolia*, S. *emodi*, S. *pubescens* subsp. *julianae*, S. *meyeri*, S. x *persica* and S. *yunnanensis*.

In 1994, several United States Department of Agriculture scientists experimented with environmentally friendly products to control powdery mildew. Their best results came from horticultural oils sprayed twice between July and September, the second time four weeks after the first. They sprayed between 10 a.m. and 2 p.m. using the products Sunspray Ultra-Fine and Saf-T-Side. Sodium bicarbonate (baking soda), which has proved an effective fungicide on some shrubs, including roses and euonymus, did not work on lilacs.

Virus: Ring spot produces yellow or target spots on the leaves, which drop early. The plant eventually dies.

There is no cure: affected plants should be destroyed.

Wilt: Although fairly unusual, verticillium wilt can affect lilacs planted in soil where tomatoes, potatoes or eggplants formerly grew. Sudden wilting may affect one branch or one side of the plant. Eventually, the entire plant will die, so it should be removed. Wilt is difficult to control, so take care when choosing a planting site.

Pests

Lilac borers: Most common east of the Rockies, these troublesome grubs are the larvae of *Podosesia syringae* var. *syringae*, a wasplike moth with translucent brownish wings. In late spring, it lays masses of eggs on stems of lilac and ash. The hatching larvae tunnel into the branches and feed on the wood. The first time you'll likely notice the infestation is when all the leaves on

Old growth is the most likely candidate for poor blooming and susceptibility to pests such as scale and borers.

an entire stem or branch turn yellow and wilt, usually in spring or early summer. Large branches may swell and crack. Look closely, and you'll see small holes about the diameter of a pencil lead a foot or two (30-60 cm) above the ground. Directly underneath, you'll see a small amount of sawdust. The small holes are exit wounds, so the perpetrators have already left, but chances are, more are at work. When you prune, you may see the borer tunnel penetrating the heart-wood of older branches.

Borers are most common on stressed and wounded plants and on large, older shoots, especially on *S. vulgaris*. There are pesticides labeled for lilac borer.

Dave Bakker, retired propagation manager of J.C. Bakker & Sons Nurseries in Canada, says he sees much less evidence of lilac borer now than he did 25 or 30 years ago. "People would say, 'I've got sawdust at the bottom of my lilac, what do I do?'" Bakker speculates that after the banning of DDT, an increase in the bird population may have lowered the number of borers.

Lilac leaf miners: The larvae of a small moth species (*Caloptilia syringella*), leaf miners tunnel between the layers of the leaves, making the leaves look blotched in early summer. They then roll the leaves and feed externally. Leaves eventually turn brown, so the entire plant may look burned. When the leaves first show signs of injury, they can be drenched with a nicotine spray or neem, but once the damage is noticed, it is generally too late to take action. Remove affected leaves, and keep the area under the shrubs clear of leaves in fall to prevent reinfection. The damage is more aesthetic than physiological. *S. vulgaris* is especially susceptible to leaf miners, and they are more problematic in certain areas such as the West Coast.

A lilac borer hole on a branch indicates that the pest has exited, but there are likely more at work, eating their way up through the center of the branch, ABOVE. *Pruning of diseased wood leads to full bloom of 'St. Joan,'* FACING PAGE, *the following year.*

Mites: The eriophyid mite (*Aculus massalongoi*) produces a silver or rust color on lilac leaves and may cause some leaf-rolling.

Oyster shell scale: Scales are odd insects; they look like flat, oval, lifeless bumps. What they do is extract fluid from the plant while they protect themselves under a waxy coating. They lay their eggs on the bark in fall or spring, and the eggs hatch in late spring. The young scales, which are pale yellow or orange, are mobile and only about 0.1 inch (2 mm) long. Once they find a place to feed, their legs wither. What you may first notice, probably while pruning, are stems that look unusually gray and roughened. Look closely, and you will see small bumps that can be scraped off with a fingernail or the blade of your pruning shears.

Lepidosaphes ulmi, the type of scale that infests lilacs, can be controlled by pruning out the most heavily infested branches and then applying a dormant-oil spray the next spring before the leaves have developed. This treatment should take place before bud break on a dry, sunny, mild morning. To prevent injury to the plant, do not apply within 48 hours of a frost or at a temperature lower than 39 degrees F (4°C). If possible, choose a calm morning when the temperature is above 60 degrees F (15°C) and frost is not forecast for that night. Scale can also be killed by a lime-sulfur solution painted directly on the branches or by direct contact with a spray of soapy water: a teaspoon (5 mL) of an additive-free liquid dish soap such as Ivory to a quart (1 L) of water. This soap spray is most effective in late spring and early summer, when scales are at the crawler stage. Spray until the foliage drips.

Sources

INTERNATIONAL MAIL ORDER— UNITED STATES AND CANADA

These sources will ship beyond their borders. When ordering plants from a nursery outside your own country, you must be prepared to fill out importation forms from your own federal department of agriculture. The importation of lilacs is restricted in some states, so you may be required to order from your own area in California, Washington, Oregon, Arizona, Nevada, Utah, New Mexico and Idaho.

ARBORVILLAGE
Box 227
Holt, MO 64048 USA
(816) 264-3911; fax: (816) 264-3760
e-mail: arborvillage@aol.com
www.nurseryman.com/searchdata/arborvillage.html
Approximately 70 lilacs, including a good selection of Fiala releases.

CONGDON & WELLER NURSERY, INC.
Box 1507
Mile Block Road
North Collins, NY 14111 USA
(716) 337-0171; fax: (716) 337-0203
e-mail: joefortune@aol.com
www.goldenlilacs.com

CORN HILL NURSERIES LTD.
R.R. 5
Petitcodiac, NB, Canada E0A 2H0
(506) 756-3635; fax: (506) 756-1087
Approximately 18 lilacs. Catalog free.

FORESTFARM
990 Tetherow Road
Williams, OR 97544 USA
(541) 846-7269; fax: (541) 846-6963
e-mail: forestfarm@rvi.net
www.forestfarm.com
60 to 70 lilacs. Catalog $5.

GREAT PLANT COMPANY
e-mail: plants@greatplants.com
www.greatplants.com
Select Plus lilacs available over the Internet.

GREER GARDENS
1280 Goodpasture Island Road
Eugene, OR 97401 USA
(541) 686-8266 or (800) 541-0111;
fax: (931) 686-0910
e-mail: orders@greergardens.com
www.greergardens.com
Catalog free.

HORTICO INC.
723 Robson Road, R.R. 1
Waterdown, ON, Canada L0R 2H1
(905) 689-6984; fax: (905) 689-6566
e-mail: hortico@bigwave.ca
www.hortico.com
Shrubs and trees catalog $3.

SELECT PLUS INTERNATIONAL NURSERY
1510 Pine
Mascouche, PQ, Canada J7L 2M4
(514) 477-3797
www.spi.8m.com
Informative website. Approximately 950 lilacs.

MAIL ORDER—CANADA ONLY

These sources ship only to Canadian addresses. Some Canadian sources are also listed above under International Mail Order.

HOLE'S GREENHOUSES & GARDENS LTD.
101 Bellerose Drive
St. Albert, AB T8N 8N8
(403) 419-6800; fax: (403) 459-6042
e-mail: info@holesonline.com
www.holesonline.com
Approximately 21 lilacs, including some standards.

SKINNER'S NURSERY AND GARDEN CENTRE LTD.
Box 220
Roblin, MB R0L 1P0
(204) 564-2336; fax: (204) 564-2324
e-mail: mail@skinnersnursery.mb.ca
www.skinnersnursery.mb.ca
Approximately 14 lilacs, including releases by Frank Skinner.

MAIL ORDER— UNITED STATES ONLY

These sources ship only to U.S. addresses. See also International Mail Order, above. Note that in the southern states, local sources of lilacs are scarce because most of these shrubs will not flower where winters are warm. If necessary, check the list of species and varieties most likely to succeed in the south before ordering from one of the northern suppliers. Importation is restricted in some states.

COLLINS LILAC HILL NURSERY
2366 Turk Hill Road
Victor, NY 14564
(716) 223-1669
More than 200 lilacs from Ted "Doc Lilac" Collins.

COUNTRY LACE LILACS
10202 NE 279th Street
Battle Ground, WA 98604
(206) 687-1874

FOX HILL NURSERY
347 Lunt Road
Freeport, ME 04032
Phone/fax: (207) 729-1511
e-mail: info@lilacs.com
www.lilacs.com
More than 90 lilacs. Catalog free.

HULDA KLAGER LILAC GARDENS
115 S. Pekin Road
Woodland, WA 98674
(360) 225-8996
www.lilacgardens.com/catalog.html

RIDGEWOOD FARMS
661 McQuade Circle
Micminnville, TN 37110
(931) 939-2258; fax: (931) 939-2009
www.tnnursery.com/Ridgewood

WAYSIDE GARDENS
1 Garden Lane
Hodges, SC 29695
(800) 213-0379
www.waysidegardens.com
Approximately 17 lilacs. Catalog free or order online.

NO MAIL ORDER—
UNITED STATES AND CANADA

BLUM RANCH
31880 Aliso Canyon Road
Acton, CA 93510 USA
(661) 947-2796
e-mail: BlumRanch@aol.com
Four acres of lilacs at a 3,000-foot elevation.

HEARD GARDENS LTD.
8000 Raccoon River Drive
West Des Moines, IA 50266 USA
(515) 987-0800; fax: (515) 987-0801
www.heardgardens.com
Approximately 40 lilacs. Website includes a lilac
Q&A.

HUMBER NURSERIES LTD.
R.R. 8
Brampton, ON, Canada L6T 3Y7
(416) 798-8733; fax: (905) 794-1311
e-mail: humber@gardencentre.com
www.gardencentre.com

KING'S TREE FARM & NURSERY
44 Belvedere Road
Boxford, MA 01921 USA
(978) 352-6359; fax: (978) 352-3313
More than 50 lilacs.

LAKE STREET GARDEN CENTER
37 Lake Street
Salem, NH 03079 USA
(603) 893-5858; fax: (603) 893-5217
www.lakestreet.com
Approximately 60 lilac varieties. Display gardens.

RABBIT RUN NURSERY
224 North Avenue
Rochester, MA 02770-1847 USA
(508) 763-2009
Approximately 18 lilacs.

SYRINGA PLUS
Box 363
44 Belvedere Road
West Boxford, MA 01885 USA
(978) 352-3301; fax: (978) 352-3313
e-mail: SyringaEvR@aol.com
More than 50 lilacs.

TWOMBLY NURSERY
163 Barn Hill Road
Monroe, CT 06468 USA
(203) 261-2133; fax: (203) 261-9230
e-mail: info@twomblynursery.com
www.twomblynursery.com
Approximately 50 lilacs.

WEDGE NURSERY
R.R. 2, Box 114
Albert Lea, MN 56007 USA
(507) 373-5225
Approximately 140 lilacs.

WESTON NURSERIES
East Main Street (Route 135)
Box 186
Hopkinton, MA 01748 USA
(508) 435-3414; fax: (508) 435-3274
www.westonnurseries.com
Wholesaler with one retail outlet, 25 lilacs

PUBLIC LILAC COLLECTIONS— CANADA

ALBERTA
Devonian Botanic Garden
Devon, AB
For information, contact:
University of Alberta
Edmonton, AB T6G 2E1

Alberta Agriculture Research Station
Brooks, AB
(403) 362-3391

MANITOBA
Agriculture Canada Research Station
Morden, MB R0G 1J0
(204) 822-7201; fax: (204) 822-7209
e-mail: cdavidson@em.agr.ca
http://res2.agr.ca/winnipeg/overmor.htm
Around 300 accessions of lilac open to the public
during business hours.

ONTARIO
Arboretum
Central Experimental Farm
Prince of Wales Drive
Ottawa, ON
www.agr.ca
Approximately 250 named cultivars, including a Lilac
Walk in the Ornamental Garden.

The Arboretum
University of Guelph
Guelph, ON N1G 2W1
(519) 824-4120 ext. 2113; fax: (519) 763-9598
e-mail: arboretu@uguelph.ca
www.uoguelph.ca/~arboretu
Historic lilac collection. Approximately 67 selections
representing 20 species.

Royal Botanical Gardens
Box 399
Hamilton, ON L8N 3H8
www.rbg.ca
With more than 800 cultivars, the Katie Osborne
Lilac Garden is one of the world's largest collections.
It is presented beautifully in a valley surrounded by
woodlands. Lilac Festival in late May.

QUEBEC
Montreal Botanical Garden
4101 Rue Sherbrooke Est
(Pie IX Metro Station)
Montreal, PQ H1X 2B2
(514) 872-1400

PUBLIC LILAC COLLECTIONS— UNITED STATES

CALIFORNIA
Descanso Gardens
1418 Descanso Drive
La Canada Flintridge, CA 91011
(818) 952-4400
www.descansogardens.com
160 acres of show gardens 20 minutes from downtown
Los Angeles include a warm-climate lilac collection
best viewed in March.

COLORADO
Denver Botanic Garden
1005 York Street
Denver, CO
(720) 865-3632; fax: (720) 865-3683
www.botanicgardens.org
More than 130 different types of lilac in the garden
and at Chatfield Nature Preserve, which is pioneering
growing lilacs at mile-high elevations and in a climate
of low rainfall, necessitating artificial irrigation.

IDAHO
University of Idaho Arboretum and Botanical Garden
Moscow, ID 83843
(208) 885-6250; fax: (208) 885-4040
www.uidaho.edu
Syringa vulgaris planted according to bloom color;
also other hybrids and species.

ILLINOIS
The Morton Arboretum
4100 Illinois Route 53
Lisle, IL 60532-1293
This lilac collection was started in the 1920s and has
been moved and renovated a number of times. The arboretum does not have a formally named lilac collection now but concentrates most of its 350 plants in a
series of beds in Godshawk Meadow, a landscaped
area. Others are distributed throughout various collections and landscaped plantings.

IOWA
Ewing Park
McKinley Road and Indianola Road
Des Moines, IA
Information from:
Department of Parks and Recreation
City of Des Moines
3226 University
Des Moines, IA 50311
(515) 271-4700
www.ci.des-
moines.ia.us/departments/pr/parkshelter.htm
The Lilac Arboretum includes about 1,400 plants.
Lilac Sunday in May.

Stampe Lilac Garden
Duck Creek Park
3300 E. Locust Street
Davenport, IA
(319) 326-7894 or (319) 326-7818
A small lilac garden popular for wedding photographs.

KANSAS
Bartlett Arboretum
State Route 55 just off I-35
Box 38
Belle Plaine, KS 67013
(316) 488-3451
Collection of early-blooming shrubs and trees includes
lilacs.

MAINE
McLaughlin Garden
Box 16
South Paris, ME 04281
(207) 743-8820
www.mclaughlingarden.org
More than 100 different lilacs. Lilac Festival on the
first Saturday in June.

MASSACHUSETTS
The Arnold Arboretum
126 Arborway
Jamaica Plain, MA 02130
(617) 524-1718
e-mail: arbweb@arnarb.harvard.edu
www.arboretum.harvard.edu
The best lilac collection in the United States, with
more than 500 plants, including about 190 cultivars
and 23 species and their botanical varieties. Associated with Harvard University. Lilac Sunday in May.

MICHIGAN
Mackinac Island, MI
(800) 4 LILACS
www.mackinacisland.org or www.mackinac.com
Ten-day lilac festival every year in June.

MINNESOTA
Minnesota Landscape Arboretum
3675 Arboretum Drive
Chanhassen, MN 55317
(612) 443-2460
Around 150 lilacs bloom in early May. Phone for dates
and directions.

NEBRASKA
Earl Maxwell Arboretum
University of Nebraska
East Campus
Lincoln, NE
(402) 472-2679

NEW HAMPSHIRE
Wentworth-Coolidge Mansion
Portsmouth, NH
(603) 436-6607
The Wentworth-Coolidge Lilac Festival includes
tours and propagation of clones of the original *Syringa
vulgaris* cultivars grown here in the 18th century.

NEW JERSEY
Alice Harding Memorial Lilac Walk
Rutgers Display Gardens
Cook College, Rutgers University
Ryders Lane, U.S. Hwy 1
North Brunswick, NJ 08901
(732) 932-8451; fax: (732) 932-7060
e-mail: rugardens@aesop.rutgers.edu
http://aesop.rutgers.edu/~rugardens
Around 100 cultivars in a collection named for the
author of *Lilacs in My Garden* (Macmillan, 1933).

NEW YORK
Brooklyn Botanical Garden
Louisa Clark Spencer Lilac Collection
1000 Washington Avenue
Brooklyn, NY 11225
www.bbg.org
Includes 21 species and 130 cultivars.

George Landis Arboretum
Lape Road
Box 186
Esperance, NY 12066
(518) 875-6935
www.townofesperance.org/nonprft.htm
Lilac collection including the releases of Fred Lape.

Highland Park
Lilac Festival
171 Reservoir Avenue
Rochester, NY 14620
(716) 256-4960
e-mail: lilacfestival@roch.com
www.roch.com/lilacfestival
More than 500 cultivars of lilac. Annual 10-day
Lilac Festival in late May.

OHIO
Holden Arboretum
9500 Sperry Road
Kirtland, OH 44094-5172
(440) 946-4400
e-mail: holden@holdenarb.org
www.holdenarb.org
The Lilac Demonstration Garden includes about
260 plants.

PENNSYLVANIA
Swarthmore College
500 College Avenue
Swarthmore, PA 19081-1390
(610) 328-8025; for directions: (610) 328-8001
e-mail: scott@swarthmore.edu
www.scottarboretum.org
The Arthur H. Scott Horticultural Foundation Lilac
Collection
includes 160 lilac plants representing 90 taxa.

UTAH
Utah Botanical Gardens
1817 N. Main Street
Farmington, UT 84025
(801) 451-3204
Lilac collection in this garden, which is about 20 miles
(32 km) south of Salt Lake City.

VIRGINIA
Meadowlark Botanical Gardens
9750 Meadowlark Gardens Court
Vienna, VA 22182
(703) 255-2621
e-mail: meadowlark@starpower.net

WASHINGTON
John A. Finch Arboretum
W. 3404 Woodland Boulevard
Spokane, WA
(509) 747-2894
More than 75 *Syringa* cultivars located in
southwest Spokane.

Hulda Klager Lilac Gardens
Box 828
115 South Pekin Road
Woodland, WA 98674
(306) 225-8996
The "Lilac Lady's" garden, about 30 miles (50 km)
north of Portland, Oregon, is a National Historic Site.
Lilac Week (actually 2 weeks) varies with the season.
Take exit 21 off I-5.

Spokane Lilac Association
Annual Lilac Festival
e-mail: office@lilacfestival.org
www.lilacfestival.org
The Grand Lilac Parade is the third Saturday in May
at 7:30 p.m.

WISCONSIN
Longnecker Gardens
University of Wisconsin Arboretum
1207 Seminole Hwy
Madison, WI 53711-3726
(608) 263-7888; fax: (608) 262-5209
www.wiscinfo.doit.wisc.edu/arboretum
One of the country's largest displays of lilacs,
Longnecker Gardens lies along the southern half
of Lake Wingra.

INFORMATION WEBSITES

*See also the websites of the lilac sources and gardens
mentioned above.*

http//lilacs.freeservers.com
Website of the International Lilac Society; links to
other lilac sites.

www.arborquest.com
Some plant descriptions.

www.ars.org/publications/heat_zone_map.htm
Climatic heat zones for the United States.

www.baileynursery.com
e-mail: plants@baileynursery.com
This wholesaler tells you where to buy their lilacs and
gives detailed descriptions of the 47 types they sell.

www.lewisriver.com/lilacs.html
Information about Hulda Klager Lilac Gardens; links
to other lilac sites.

www. members.tripod.com/Hatch_L/syringa.html
Freek Vrugtmann's list of lilacs and where to purchase
them.

www.fourseasonsnursery.com
Wholesale only, but they provide some good lilac
descriptions.

www.lilacgifts.com
Website for souvenirs associated with the Rochester
Lilac Festival.

www.monrovia.com
Wholesale only, but they will tell you where to buy
their plants, and there are descriptions and photos
of their 14 or so lilacs.

www.usna.usda.gov
Website of the United States Department of Agriculture arboretum in Washington, DC.

This simplified version of the U.S. Department of Agriculture's latest climatic-zone map indicates general temperature trends throughout Canada and the United States. The temperature ranges indicate average minimum winter temperatures. Colder zones have lower numbers. Nursery catalogs usually indicate the coldest zone in which a plant will thrive. Plants that are successful in your zone and in zones with numbers lower than yours should survive winters in your garden. Plants that prefer zones with higher numbers than yours may not be winter-hardy for you.

Zone 1
Below –50°F
Below –45°C

Zone 2
–50 to –40°F
–45 to –40°C

Zone 3
–40 to –30°F
–40 to –35°C

Zone 4
–30 to –20°F
–35 to –29°C

Zone 5
–20 to –10°F
–29 to –23°C

Zone 6
–10 to 0°F
–23 to –18°C

Zone 7
0 to 10°F
–18 to –12°C

Zone 8
10 to 20°F
–12 to –6°C

Zone 9
20 to 30°F
–6 to –1°C

Zone 10
30 to 40°F
–1 to 4.5°C

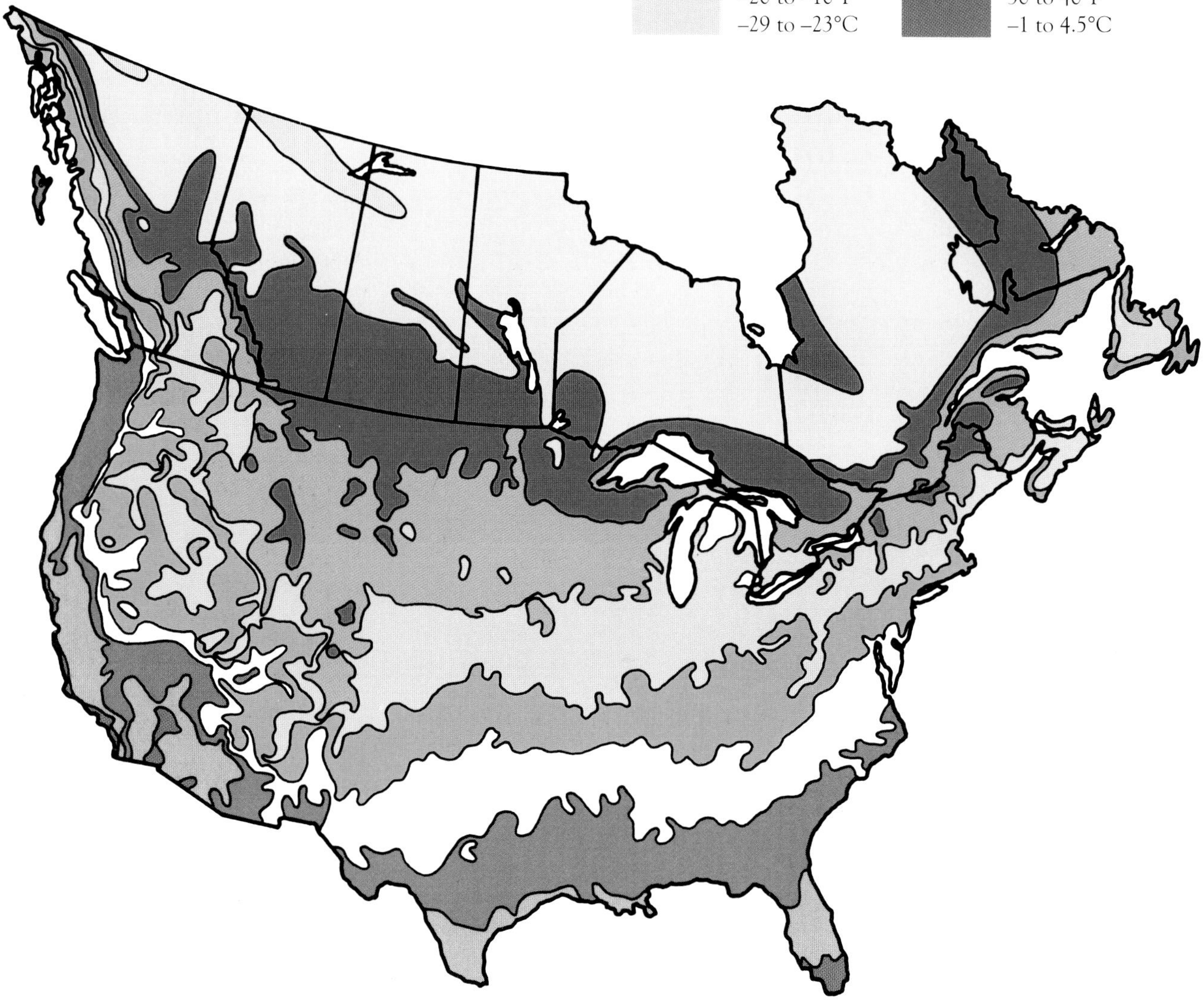

Index

Credits

All photographs © Jennifer Bennett, with the exception of those that appear on the following pages:

21, 33, 38, 44, 51, 98, 104, 109: Photographs © Turid Forsyth

23: Photograph © John Ruskay

25: Illustration from *Paradisi in Sole, Paradisus Terrestris* by John Parkinson (1629)

36: Illustration courtesy Agriculture Canada

A special thanks to copy editor and indexer Mary Patton for her work on this project, to Angelo Varriano and Dr. Louis Kennedy for their lilacs and to Bruce Peart of the Royal Botanical Gardens.